HOW TO USE RADAR

HOW TO
USE RADAR
—— H. G. Strepp ——

Published by Nautical Books
an imprint of
A & C Black (Publishers) Ltd
35 Bedford Row, London WC1R 4JH

© Klasing & Co Gmbh

© English Language text Nautical Books
1990

ISBN 0 7136 3324 7

A CIP catalogue record for this book is
available from the British Library.

Translated from the German Edition by
Robin Inches, MITI.

Photographs: Gert B. Büttgenbach, H. G.
Strepp, Decca,
Wasserschutzpolizei Kiel, Furono (UK) Ltd.

Printed in Great Britain by St Edmundsbury Press Ltd
Bury St Edmunds, Suffolk

Contents

Preface

My first book about compact radars for yachts and other small craft has, thanks to Poseidon, been sold out for some time, and anyway today's small-craft radars are different, although the new ones do not, and indeed cannot, give as detailed a picture as did the viewing screens that had to have a light-excluding hood fitted in daylight. Today's sets can be looked at, by several people at once, in daylight or at night, and in the better sets that advantage outweighs the inevitable loss of information introduced by the digitalised video technique.

Unfortunately, however, there are now also mini-radars that are useful for charming the money out of the pockets of sailors, but useless for finding the entrance to a fishing harbour even from a mile out.

The primary purpose of radar is to prevent collisions at sea — yet it has often led to such. Radar is a useful navigation aid, even when the visibility is excellent, because on board small craft it usually allows one to take bearings somewhat more accurately than with pelorus or bearing compasses, and one can then straightaway read off the length of the bearing line. Gert Büttgenbach, who runs radar courses between Wilhelmshaven and Heligoland, has kindly contributed the photographs.

Hans G. Strepp

About Your Equipment

The Physics

The radar sends out a rapid succession of short pulses or high-frequency electromagnetic waves whose velocity of propagation is around 300,000 km/s, i.e. approximately the speed of light. If such a pulse encounters an obstacle it is reflected, and surface elements perpendicular to the direction of the pulse-beam send an echo back to the transmitting aerial. This has in the meantime been changed over to the receiving, and passes the echo on to the receiver, where the time interval between pulse emission and echo return is measured and multiplied by the speed of light to obtain the length of the two-way pulse path.

The pulse frequency of small-craft radars is around 9 Gc/s (Giga = a thousand million), pulse duration less than 1μs (microseconds; Micro = a millionth) and pulse repetition frequency in the region of 820–920/s.

The pulse power input should not be less than 3 kW; the energy consumption (kWh = kilowatt-hours) is nevertheless tolerable because the pulses produced by the radar transmitter are so extremely brief.

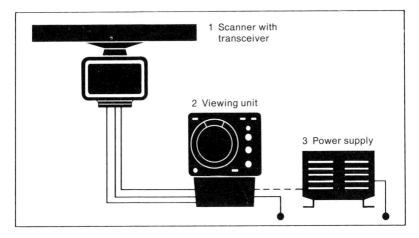

1 Scanner with transceiver

2 Viewing unit

3 Power supply

Fig. 1

The Transceiver

This is the most important and most expensive part of the radar installation, and is housed in the casing, on top of which the aerial rotates, usually at 24–29 rpm.

In the prospectus, important technical data as regards the transmitter are: power, pulse duration and, because it belongs to it, the rotating aerial. Transmission frequency, usually stated in megahertz (MHz), and whether the transmitting/receiving changeover is achieved by means of a magnetron or a Gunn-oscillator, is not important.

Transmitter Power

Three kW is enough power for small yacht-radars whose range is limited to 16 nm or less. For longer ranges you need 10kW (40–70 nm) or 25 kW (up to 100 nm).

Pulse Duration

For close range, pulse duration should not be more than 0/08 microseconds, since otherwise you cannot distinguish between objects in line and less than 13 m (43 ft). apart. However, pulse duration must be increased for greater distances, since otherwise too little of the transmission gets back. For a range of 6–60 nm, 0.6 microseconds are usual; for even longer ranges, 1.2 microseconds.

Pulse duration is normally set automatically as the range is varied, and the more pulse-duration steps there are, the better the set. To be able to alter the pulse duration at will, for instance to penetrate further into a wall of rain, you have to have what amounts almost to a 'professional' set.

The Aerial

With few exceptions, radar aerials these days are slot radiators, and for yachts, rarely longer than 5 m (16 ft); hidden beneath a hood (radome) permeable to radio waves. This permits a horizontal concentration of the radar beam down to 4° (= 0.070 rad). The radian as an angular measure is as practical in navigation as it is disliked because unfamiliar; what it means here is that the radar lobe 4° wide horizontally shows every point target as an arc of 0.07 × its distance. A small buoy 1000 m distant is thus seen by this 4° aerial as an object 70 m (230 ft) wide, and shown that size, appropriately scaled down, on the screen. A harbour entrance 100 m (328 ft) wide is already barely recognisable at 1 km (0.5 nm) distance. This length of aerial represents the lowest level of compromise still acceptable.

Wherever possible, even if it does not look very smart, you should pick a 1.2 m (4 ft) aerial with 1.8° (0.031 rad), or a 1.83 m (6 ft) one with 1.2° (0.021 rad). To be allowed to sail on the Rhine in fog with radar, you are required to fit an 2.4 m (8 ft) long aerial (0.017 rad).

The vertical angle of departure of radar aerials is usually 25°, to ensure that echoes come back and are detected even when the vessel is rolling.

Aerial mounting height

If the aerial is at a height of h/m above the water, then the horizon for it is $2.2 \sqrt{h}$ nautical miles away — even cheap pocket calculators should be able to work that out. If calculation is too laborious for you, you can look in the table for 'dip of sea horizon' in the List of Lights or a nautical almanac; the difference between a light beam and a radar beam is minimal.

An aerial at a height of 5 m (16 ft) sees the horizon at a distance of 4.92 nm, but that is no reason for having a radar with only limited range. It is simply that the aerial is too low. A radar with a long range can detect high-rise land beyond the horizon sooner than you can see it.

The Display Unit

Now and then at boat shows you still see sets with fluorescent-screen tubes that you can look at only if there is no light falling on to the screen. That is tedious in daylight, particularly for those wearing spectacles, because nose and eyes have to be poked into a viewing-hood mounted above the screen; however, this technique has the advantage of optimum picture definition without loss of information.

Prevalent nowadays for small radars is the daylight VDU (visual display unit) and raster scan technique. 'Raster' here means a picture built up from dots; 'scan' means 'to traverse by controlled beam'. The radar aerial is frequently called the 'scanner'. As regards scanning by the aerial, there is no difference between what happens with raster scan and what happened previously, but its display is different.

On the CRT (cathode ray tube) screen the picture is built up using polar coordinates — angle and radius. Anyone with a little understanding of maths knows that you can convert polar coordinates into cartesian ones — height and width. So-called scientific pocket calculators are also able to do this, and so are the display units of modern small radars. Thus their picture is built up horizontally line-by-line from a multitude of spots, single- or multi-coloured, comparable to that on the monitor of a computer.

This has produced a second resolution criterion for modern small radars: the fineness of the raster — or the number of spots in the X-direction (line) and the number in the Y-direction (height) of the screen. 500×500 is considered the minimum requirement, but there are differing figures such as 512×620 where the screen is rectangular, stood on end. This does not affect the real radar information (i.e. distance rings remain rings) but provides larger corners for supplementary information — more about that directly. Of course you cannot count the spots, but you can look at the VRM (variable range marker) or the fixed range markers. The screen is OK if you can observe the stepped structure of the rings only by studying it closely under a glass.

With a square or rectangular video-screen, the manufacturers obligingly copy-on special information alphanumerically (letters and digits); such as what range the VRM indicates and the relative bearing of the electronic bearing marker (EBM), the range selected, and the ship's position coordinates or time difference hyperbola (TD) according to Loran C.

Currently, most small radars are head-up unstabilised (i.e. the heading marker points towards the bow of the boat), but developments are in hand to link the fluxgate compass to the radar.

What is quite certain is that some day both the new satellite navigation system GPS, which has been significantly delayed by NASA's rocket failures, and the electronic chart will be coupled to small radars. But there is no sense in waiting until the perfect system is available; that never happens anyway, because development is always continuing.

But do beware of the bad advice that a poor, indeed an unsuitable, set is better than none at all. It is better to be ultra-careful through being blind than to be too dashing with a sort of radar-with-cataract.

There are very modern sets on the market where everything is touch-activated, even taking a bearing; radar veterans prefer to rotate knobs and consider that more sensitive — perhaps because that is what we have always been accustomed to. Both versions are on the market. There are also small radars with kinescope, and these are thoroughly modern sets. Colour sets are intended to help with a particular difficulty with navigation by radar: the differentiation of weak and strong echoes. What is beach and what cliff? The Japanese started it — weak echo yellow or orange, strong echo red, background adjustable between blue and black, rings and bearing line green. I also thought this a good idea when it first appeared, but practical experience has shown this colourfulness to be tiring. Too much colour covers the screen with daubs and blurs the contours. Monochrome on a black background is clearer and is

Control Symbols and Abbreviations

Off

Stand by

On, Transmit

Tuning

Brilliance, Brightness

Gain

Heading Marker

Bearing Marker, Cursor

Anti-Clutter Rain, Minimum and Maximum

Anti-Clutter Sea, Minimum and Maximum

Range Rings Brilliance

Variable Range Marker (VRM)

Short, Long Pulse

Aerial Rotating

North Up Presentation

Other designations on the set

CRT — Cathode Ray Tube
FTC — Fast Time Control
Head-up — Set up for Relative Bearings
PPI — Plan Position Indicator
PRF—Pulse Repetition Frequency
STC — Sensitivity Time Control
XMTR — Transmitter

standard among professionals; it is only laymen who are capti-
vated by colours.

Switching the display unit on and off frequently, shortens the
life of the screen. That should be a warning to thrifty skippers and
also owners of personal computers.

Special Case — Sailing Boats

Three kW of transmitter power can adequately be supplied by the
engine-driven generator, but of course the engine has to be running. The other problem for cruisers of up to about 9 m (30 ft) in
length, is the radar scanner with the transceiver. The smallest
radome has a diameter of 45 cm (18 in) and weighs 5 kg (11 lb), but
with a horizontal angle of 6° the scanner is too small. With a screen
of 500 × 500 instead of 128 × 128 offered, it would perhaps be better
than nothing! Furuno offer sailing boats a radome weighing 4.5 kg
(10 lb), together with a 490 × 656 screen, 16 nm nominal range,
VRM, EBM, alarm, unwanted-echo suppression and alpha-
numeric notices in the corners of the display unit. That was the
'state of the art' at the time of writing.

Images

The images that appear on the screen are not always as obvious as a coastline, and need further explanation. We have read already that, because of the lobar form of the radar beam with a horizontal angular width, fine details of the seascape can become blurred into a single object.

The radar picture is a pretty abstract representation to which you have to get accustomed, and into which you have to penetrate. You can teach yourself by constantly comparing in good visibility how nature, the appropriate chart and the radar picture could fit together — in the radar picture there is usually quite a lot missing owing to the one-sided illumination of the surroundings of your own vessel at the centre of the PPI ('display', but do get accustomed to the abbreviation).

We are limiting the subject to 'radar for small craft and yachts', excluding the so-called 'mega-yachts', most of which are equipped as well as or better than merchant ships.

Accuracy of Bearings

Because a cape or a buoy is portrayed wider than it actually is, the bearing cursor has to be lined up to the middle of the image. However, the bearing cursor nowadays is an electronically generated line rotated in steps, and the statement 'accuracy of bearing' in the set description has to be understood accordingly. In a cheap set, savings have been made in this respect also and you may well find 'better than ±5°', which is a most unsatisfactory piece of information. Just one degree, better still a half, would be acceptable.

Echo markings

The appearance of coastlines, passages and harbour entrances shows up well on radar screens seen at boat shows. But beware! Most of these displays are super-tuned and you can be fairly sure that in the case of value-for-money sets, at sea the markings will be nothing like so detailed and sharp, and no amount of tuning will make them sharper.

The Pip

If a dot appears on the PPI (plan position indicator) that was not there before, this may be a contact; say the bridge of a large vessel, rising above the radar horizon. However, you can be sure about this only if in the course of ten rotations of the scanner the 'pip' has appeared three or more times.

Pips that appear on the PPI, but do so erratically, in sailor's jargon are called 'pumping echoes', the pump being the seaway which enables you to sometimes see the entire vessel, sometimes only the tops of its masts. The pip correspondingly is sometimes thicker, sometimes thinner, and a buoy in rough seas will carry on 'pumping' for quite a long time until you get close to it.

On the monochrome PPI for daylight viewing, all pips are of the same brilliance; in the picture on a CRT their brilliance varies with the strength of the echo.

Mostly a pip as seen is made up of a bunch of smaller pips, rather like a cluster of stars, because the reflection from, say, the superstructure of a vessel comes from all sorts of surfaces and angles. For that reason it is not possible to deduce the shape of a single echo from that of a pip. The pip of a passing ship changes its appearance continuously and can sometimes look as if heading straight towards you — no need to worry. Only direction and speed of movement of the pip are of significance.

False Echoes

By these are meant echoes of real objects, incorrectly generated. Fig.2 shows how, in addition to the direct echo D of the large ship, an indirect echo I can be generated on the PPI by reflection of the radar signal from (e.g.) the wall of a building near the transmitter. Because of the small difference in pulse travel time, the indirect pip appears on the PPI at the same distance but on a different bearing.

Also in this category are the multiple echoes which arise from

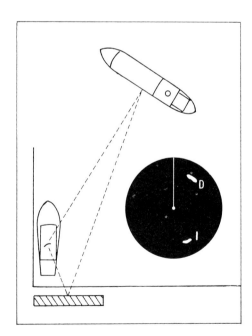

Fig. 2   Direct and indirect echo produced by beam reflection from the wall of the building.

'ping-pong effect' between quay wall and own hull (Fig.3) or another ship passing close by. The hull of a yacht or a fishing smack is too rounded to produce this effect, but we experienced something similar in the thickest of fogs off Gibraltar when we wanted to feel our way through between two large vessels at anchor. Ping-pong between those fatties completely painted over the PPI. Cure; reduce the gain.

Side Lobes

From their two ends, radar scanners additionally radiate more or less successfully damped side-lobes, which may be reflected as echoes on to the PPI from nearby targets (Fig.4). If pulse duration is too long for the distance, or the craft yaws rapidly, the side lobes may even join up with the main one to form an arc.

Ghost Echoes

These are rare and usually fleeting images, caused by the over-shoot interference with which the television-viewing public is familiar.

Unwanted Echoes

Sea clutter around your own vessel at the centre of the PPI can be very annoying. True, the somewhat larger patch to windward can to some extent be removed using the 'anti-clutter sea' knob, but that may well also remove small vessels within that area, a point which small-craft skippers should always remember before approaching a large vessel in a rough sea. Even if the big fellow has not switched on the anti-clutter, getting close in a rough sea is dangerous because the feeble pip of a small craft often does not show up against the sea-generated echoes.

Radars operating in the 9-GHz band also show up rain showers very clearly. If it is really pouring, the 'anti-clutter rain' does not achieve much any more, and to be safe one has to slow down even more than in fog.

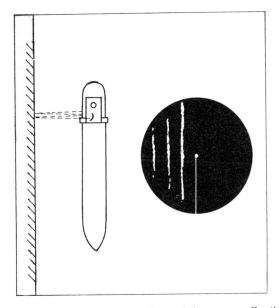

Fig. 3   Multiple echoes due to 'ping-pong effect' between quay wall and ship's side.

Fig. 4   Multiple echoes due to scanner side-loss.

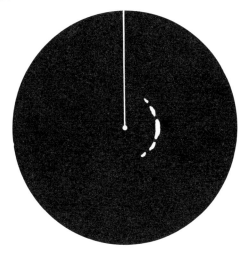

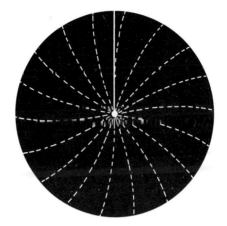

Fig. 5   Interference from other radar on same frequency.

Picture Interference

If the PPI shows slightly curved dotted lines, running towards the centre, all around the screen (Fig.5), that is not a matter of echoes but of another radar operating on the same frequency nearby — and its operator will see the same thing on his PPI. Up-to-date sets suppress that sort of interference automatically; with others, you have to put up with it for a short spell.

Target Acquisition

If h is the scanner mounting-height in metres and H the height of an adequately reflective object beyond the horizon, then the theoretical acquisition or contact distance d in nautical miles is:

$$d = 2.2 \, (\sqrt{h} + \sqrt{H})$$

A radar scanner at a height of 6 m. acquires the 12-metre high superstructure of a freighter at about 13 nm; due to variability of the weather, this calculated value may be up to $\pm$ 10% out.

The contact distance is also influenced by the shape of the target. Round and pointed bodies reflect only a small part of the incoming energy back to the scanner; the same applies to surfaces inclined strongly towards the horizontal, such as the windscreens of many motor yachts.

The figures below are reference values for a radar scanner mounted 5 m. above the waterline.

Ships

Tankers, bulk carriers, cruise liners	9–12 nm
Freighters	6–9 nm
Lightship, large buoy without Racon	4–7 nm
Trawler, coaster	3–6 nm
Metal-hull boats	3–4 nm
Wooden or plastic hulled boats	$\frac{1}{2}$–$1\frac{1}{2}$ nm
with radar reflector	2–$4\frac{1}{2}$ nm
Lifeboats, rowing boats	$\frac{1}{4}$–$\frac{1}{2}$ nm

Buoys

Large with reflector	3–5 nm
Large without reflector	2–3 nm
Medium-size fairway buoys	1–2 nm
Small fairway buoys	$\frac{1}{4}$–$\frac{1}{2}$ nm

Ice

Ice to windward is hard to pick up because the cooled air bends the radar beam upwards. Smooth ice does not produce an echo; neither do ice floes with the scanner at a height of 5 m (16 ft); Icebergs and pack-ice 2–9 nm; growlers barely out to 2 nm.

If your boat has a wooden or plastic hull and is equipped with radar, you need a radar reflector all the same.

Operating the Set

Make it a habit, after switching off the set, to turn all rotary knobs anticlockwise back to the stop. In electrical engineering, that is the zero or minimum position (differing from that of a water tap or central-heating valve). Above all, before switching on, the 'brilliance' knob should be checked again to confirm minimum setting; someone might just have played with it. Switching on with the brilliance set too high shortens the life of the PPI.

Main Switch

First set it to 'standby' for 150 sec.s ($2\frac{1}{2}$ minutes) to warm up the magnetron or Gunn diode. During this phase most sets show the heading marker on the PPI, and when it ends, the measuring scale. Then you can switch to 'on'.

Sharpness of the Image

To adjust this, switch the range to 8 nm or 12 nm, depending on what is available, then increase the brilliance until the compass rose and the notes in the corners of the screen show up clearly. Finally, turn the tuning knob to and fro experimentally until the image is at its sharpest. Usually you then also have to adjust the brilliance again.

Range Selector

The range, the next parameter to be set, at around 10 nm should also be the standard observation-range during the passage. It gives early recognition of other vessels and combines good contact with the coast at a safe distance from it. Keeping that sort of distance usually also means that the 100-m (328-ft) line is between the craft and the coast, which means one is sailing in calmer water.

Associated with every range setting there is a second figure indicating the distance in nautical miles between the fixed distance rings around the centre of the PPI. These rings can be left switched on or off; standard practice is 'on'.

Variable Range Marker (VRM)
This is a ring whose radius is infinitely adjustable, moved onto a pip or object on the PPI by means of two keys or a rocker switch. The distance of the object from your own ship (= centre of the PPI) can then be read off in one corner of the screen.

Electronic Bearing Line (EBL)
Pressing the left-hand key or rocker rotates this anticlockwise until you release the key/rocker. The right-hand key or rocker rotates it the other way, until it is pointing at the object whose bearing one wants. With user-friendly sets you do not have to read off the relative bearing from the compass rose; it is shown in the corner with the VRM reading.

Automatic Alarms
On some sets these can be fitted as extras; on others they are included in the price and you have to take them even if you do not want them. They can be set for a variety of distances; anything

then entering the guard zone sets the thing off. What none of them has is a key to switch off, when you are tempted to get your head down during the graveyard watch.

Plotter

You press the 'plot' button, and all targets moving relative to your own ship paint their wake on the PPI — unfortunately so do fixed buoys and vessels at anchor if we are under way; more about that in the next chapter. With some sets you can 'freeze' the plot — don't ever do that! Whilst gazing deep in thought, you could miss important continuing developments. The plot lines replace the afterglow tails on the CRT which allowed you to recognise the relative movement of the pips, and whose appearance is shown in some illustrations in the next chapter.

Overall, adjusting and operating raster radars is simpler than it was with earlier sets, but the precise translation of the movements on the screen into the actual ones has not become any easier.

Pulse Length

Medium-sized sets, as already in use in larger motor yachts, can for the longer range settings be switched to either short or long pulse. Short improves resolution but simultaneously reduces picture strength and range. Initial pulse switch setting should be 'long'. (For short ranges, pulse length is unalterably on automatic control; the same with small radars.)

Adjusting the Picture

Brilliance

Turn the knob clockwise far enough for the writing beam (time base) to be just visible. Switch on the rings and adjust brilliance so that these just show distinctly. Usually with a change of range the brilliance needs slight readjustment. The echo resolution should be good, but the screen must not become fogged.

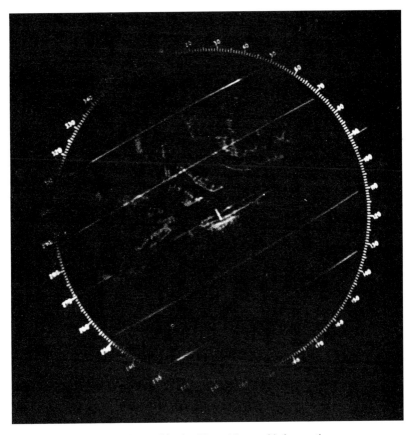

Fig. 6   Brilliance too low with significant loss of information.

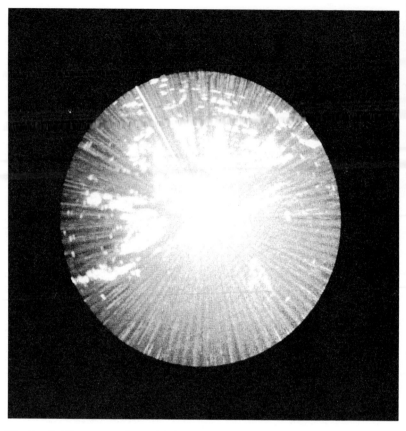

Fig. 7   Brilliance much too high; not only is there loss of
information but it also causes premature aging of display scope
luminous layer.

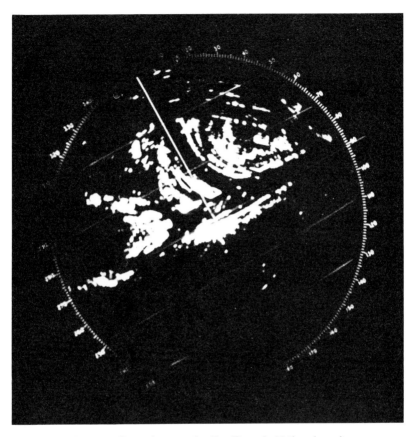

Fig. 8   Brilliance adjusted correctly. For Figs. 6–15 the rings have been switched off.

Gain

The 'gain' control adjusts the degree of signal amplification. With simple sets and older models, turn the knob clockwise until the background looks slightly gritty. With more modern sets you cannot achieve this because they have better self-noise attenuation, and excessive gain shows up as smearing-up of the picture. With sets with manual control of pulse duration, for short range take care to have this adjusted to 'short'. (All Figs. in this section were produced with a Decca Clearscan 9C.)

Insufficient gain means that weakly reflecting targets vanish, but reduction now and then can be advisable in close-range opera-

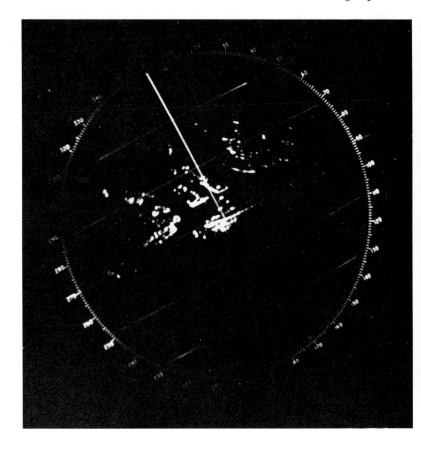

tion to fade out double echoes. Rain clutter suppression with high gain may bring up a clear picture of boundary contours on up-to-date sets, but you have to allow for a loss of information. Compare Fig.12 and Fig.10; pulse length is short in both, but Fig.12 has excessive gain, and rain clutter suppression which always swallows up weak targets. For that reason it is advisable to increase the gain a bit when suppressing rain clutter.

Fig. 9   (below left) Gain too low; low and flat targets remain invisible.

Fig. 10   (below) Gain set correctly.

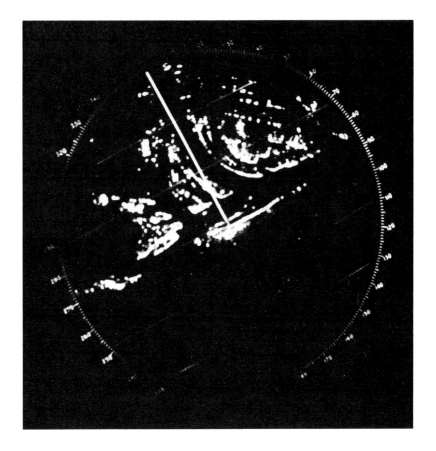

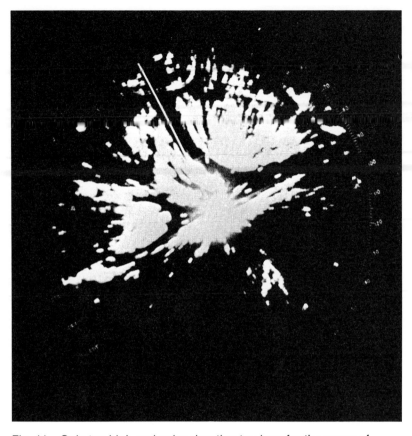

Fig. 11   Gain too high and pulse duration too long for the range of
1.5 nm.

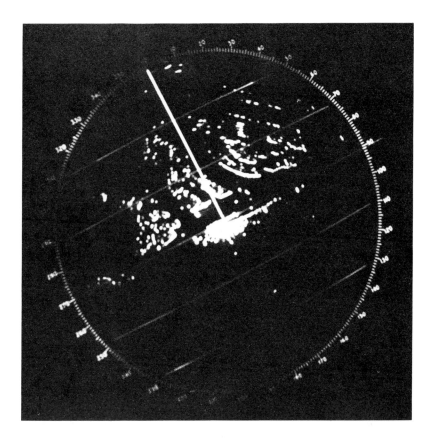

Fig. 12   Gain as in Fig. 11, but short pulse and anti-clutter rain.

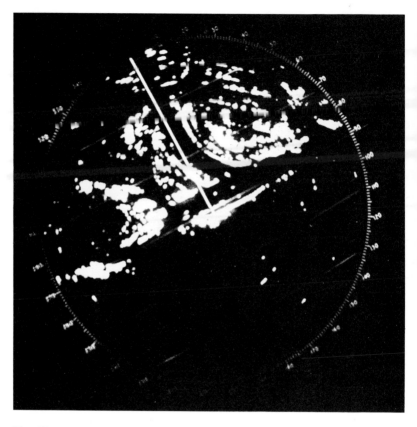

Fig. 13   As Fig. 12, but 'Clearscan 2' switched on.

Tuning

The radar set has to be tuned to the correct frequency for maximum efficiency. Turn the knob slowly through the control range until the visual readout shows a maximum. Where there is no readout, adjust to get maximum sharpness of contours; tuning should be checked periodically.

Heading Marker

Only on completion of the three above-mentioned adjustments following switching-on of the set is it worth bringing the heading marker to the zero of the bearing scale, by pressing a button several times or rotating an adjusting knob, depending on the set. If this has a movable centre, that must first be located precisely underneath the cross at the centre of the bearing dial, otherwise neither heading marker nor bearings are correct.

Anti-Clutter Gain Control, Anti-Clutter Sea

This device reduces the close-range gain, from the screen centre outwards and with diminishing effect: out at 3 or 5 nm, there is no longer any reduction of the gain set with the gain knob.

The anti-clutter gain control also removes irritating seaway echoes, but this has to be effected with care to avoid removing echoes made by contacts. When sailing in estuaries, etc., annoying multiple and side-lobe echoes can be eliminated by careful use of anti-clutter gain control, but here again one must not overdo it.

If your own ship is in a rain shower, anti-clutter gain control may (though it does not always) improve radar visibility and make strongly reflecting contacts visible again.

Anti-Clutter Rain

On some sets this is called 'differentiation'. It is infinitely adjustable and evenly effective over the whole of the screen. It is able to suppress rain, snow and hail showers to such an extent that contacts become visible again, but must not be turned up so far that useful echoes disappear. When sailing in estuaries, etc., this knob can be used to reduce the often too prominent paint of nearby targets overlapping, showing them up more clearly (Figs 14, 15).

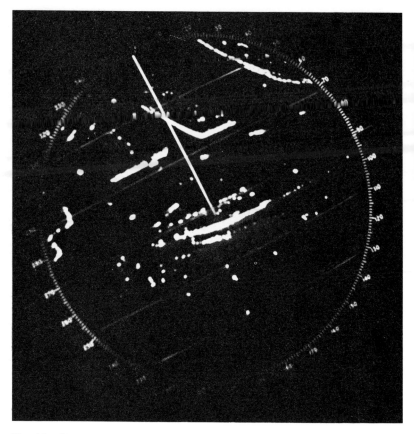

Fig. 14   Range 0.5 nm. Anti-clutter rain set halfway which is too much.

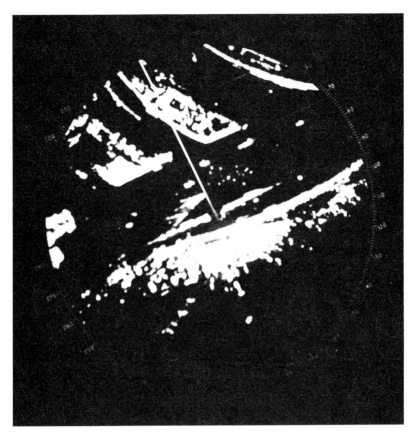

Fig. 15   Range 0.5 nm. Normal setting. Note the two bow waves to the left of the heading line.

Fig. 16   Own ship is inside a heavy shower.

Fig. 17   As a result of the correct use and continual readjustment of anti-clutter sea and anti-clutter rain, and cautious reduction of gain, the near echoes have been eliminated – but so have the ship echoes to the NE.

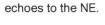

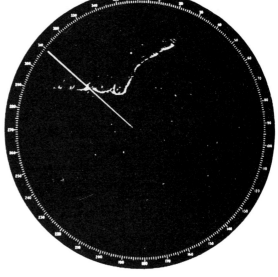

Relativity and Error

Remember: the centre of the screen is your own vessel, which is moving over the sea.

It is not only beginners who have difficulty — particularly in darkness or fog — in imagining that they are hovering vertically over their craft and are looking down on it and its surroundings, when they are looking at the PPI of their radar. All the movements which they see are, as it were, 'faked' by the movement of their own ship at the centre of the PPI; they are relative movements. A firmly anchored buoy (zero speed) which we are approaching, in the radar picture appears to be approaching us with the same speed as our own, appropriately scaled down (!). Only if your own ship is stationary does the radar picture represent reality, scaled down. The apparent immobility of the screen centre is conducive to errors.

For that reason, this is the most important chapter in this book. Do not put it down until you are quite sure you have understood everything in it. And now see to it that the heading marker is set to the zero of the bearing rose. Some sets will already have it there, with others you almost always have to zero it.

One Stationary Object plus Two Moving Ones

Fig.18a shows a developing situation as it would be portrayed on the chart. Buoy b is stationary; contact K and own ship E are in motion. Fig.18b shows the same development on the PPI, (exceptionally) to the same scale. Assume the measurements 1–4 were made at three-minute intervals. The plotter would draw two lines, one through the contact points 1–4, the other through the apparent course of the buoy. Check how this development ends, if neither vessel makes any alteration. On the PPI it looks as if around position 1, K clobbered the buoy; however, since the buoy is still there later on that was probably not the case.

In Fig.19 we first keep our own boat stationary and let the other

Fig. 18   The actual development of an encounter (left) and its radar plot (right). The buoy (b) remains where it is, but on the radar it appears to be 'passing' with own-ship's speed on the opposite course. Using compasses and protractor, check ranges and relative bearings of contact (K) in every position, on actual-development drawing and plot.

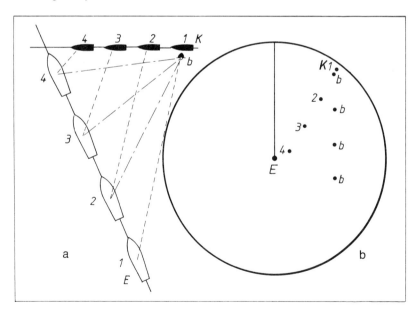

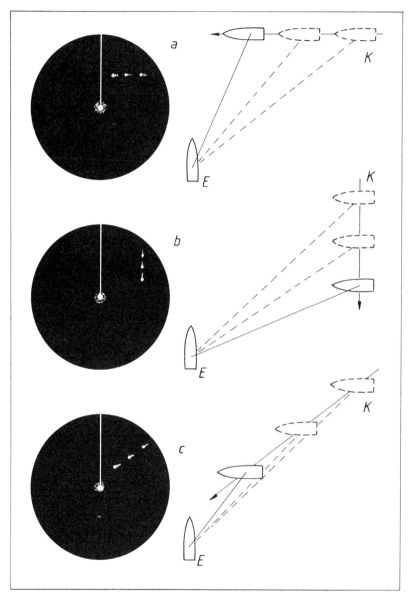

Fig. 19   (a) E stationary, K under way; (b) E under way, K stationary; (c) both under way.

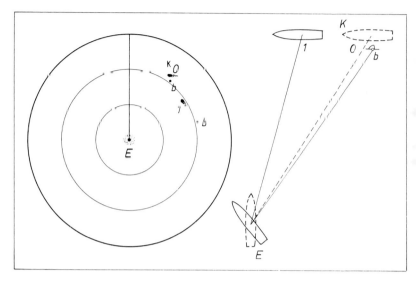

Fig. 20   Own ship (E) turning on the spot, K under way, buoy (b) stationary.

move, then the other stationary and move ourselves, and finally have both under way — and see in each case how that develops on the PPI. In the last case, a very close encounter results.

Fig.20 once more shows the buoy, and the vessel coming from the right, but this time we (E) are almost stationary but turning on the spot, 40° to port, which takes us about the same amount of time as vessel K takes to get from 0 to 1.

Taking Bearings, Measurements, Plotting

If a bearing on the radar picture remains constant, it will lead to a collision just as with a visual bearing, as Fig.21 shows, but a novice in fog at the radar would, I am sure, be astounded to see his partner in the collision emerging from the fog just like that.

It is always advisable to set the bearing line on a pip that appears, to see whether or not the bearing changes, and if so, how.

However, you do have to 'start a correspondence' (keep records) at the radar if you have to deal with several threateningly approaching pips. They have to be given names (A,B,C etc.) and their bearings and distances have to be recorded with the times, for let us not pretend — our radar is in the primitive class. It is nice that some can plot electronically, for if none of these lines points at the centre of the PPI we can set our minds at rest to some extent. Mind you, one should not let anyone get too close either; one mile from the centre is not too generous as the limiting distance for a 'close quarters' situation. To establish the course and speed of a contact, you have to plot on paper, as Fig.22 shows, for a steady relative bearing σ and a time interval of 6 min., during which the distance from the contact d → d^1 has changed. The own-ship distance-made-good in 6 min. determines the positioning of the two bearing lines.

Fig. 21   The contact is closing on a steady relative bearing of 90°.

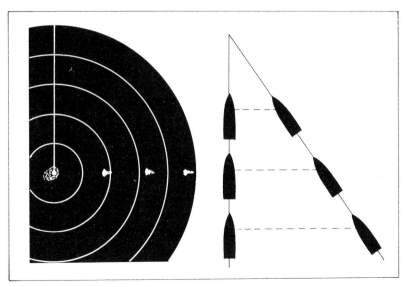

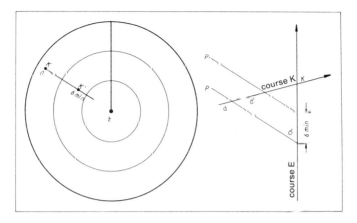

Fig. 22 Simple plot on paper (right) of what is developing on the radar screen: relative bearing σ remains steady, range d decreases.

A more practical method is to plot on a plotting sheet radar or relative motion plot (Fig.23).

As with the PPI, you show the approach of $K_1 \to K_2$, but of course that is the trace of his and our own motion combined. To identify course and speed of the contact, we draw our own distance-made-good in the time s_e parallel to the heading line backwards from K_1, and from the end-point e draw a line through K_2. That is the contact's relative course, and $e \to K_2 = s_k$ is his distance-made-good in the time; from the two his speed can be calculated. We also see not only at what angle he crosses our bows, but how far ahead he will be as indicated by the trace Sa, not by his course Sk that we have just drawn in.

Let us stay with the pre-drawn plot. K's course angle is 70° less than ours and that is the angle at which he will cross our path. Assuming we are steering 030°, then K's course is 30°–70° = −40°; since that does not appear on the compass we have to add 360°. K's compass course is 320—by our compass, of course, and with our compass error. (Well now, we do not absolutely have to know that, but it should help us to recognise how different the world of the PPI is from the real world.)

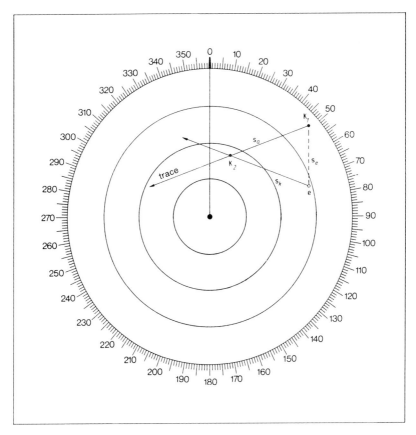

Fig. 23 $K_1 ... K_2 = S_a$, track of pip closing, over given time. S_e track of own ship, over same time. S_k track and course of contact in that time.

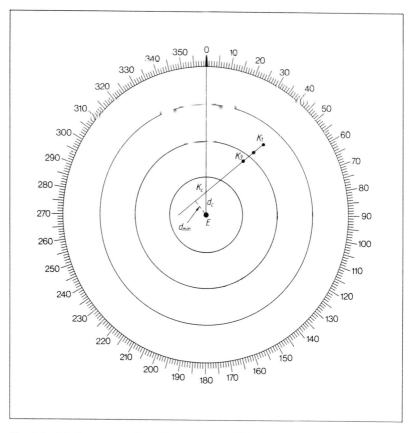

Fig. 24   Minimum passing-distance d_{min}. This is often called the CPA (closest point of approach) in radar jargon.

Minimum Passing Distance

The principle purpose of radar is to avoid collisions, and there the PPI helps us to latch on to some things more quickly.

Fig.24 shows a ship closing from starboard, i.e. with the right of way. We are the give-way boat. We plot his position three times at equal intervals of 6 min., which identifies his closing speed and trace for us. The first contact K_1 is made with relative bearing σ_1 = 40° and range 10 nm. The subsequent plottings show that K is maintaining a constant speed. Closing speed is most accurately calculated from $(K_1 \rightarrow K_3)$:12 min., retaining the dimensions nm/min. (You can work equally well with millimetres on the PPI, since the time to the crossing of the tracks can be calculated that way too.) The minimum passing distance d_{min} is that where the relative bearing line is perpendicular to the trace of the other vessel.

Since such analyses of what is happening take a certain amount of time, I expect you now understand why for general observation purposes using radar, a range setting of 8–12 nm is proposed.

Watch for Errors in Taking Bearings

Accurate bearings at a considerable distance are not exactly radar's strong point. For that reason one must try to maintain an especially steady course while a bearing is being taken, or rather read off the bearing when the helmsman reports that he is on the ordered course.

Fig.25 shows how a minor bearing error of 1.5° in the second plot can result in an erroneous analysis. If A is on a collision course, the error in the bearing at the second reading at 8 nm distance can make it look as if A were going to pass us just less than 2 nm clear, ahead or astern depending on whether the error was positive or negative. We also recognise that a bearing 'accuracy' of 3°, or even worse 5°, built into the set implies a mammoth degree of uncertainty at very short range. Do not be too optimistic; it is there alright.

In poor visibility, a minimum passing distance of 1 nm should be considered as a too-close-quarters situation, particularly with a radar from the lower end of the performance/price band.

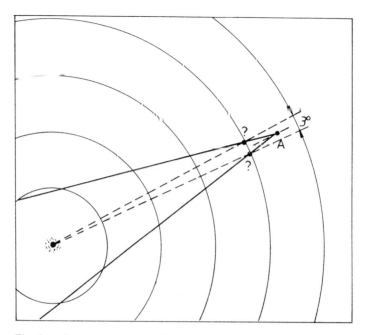

Fig. 25   Error due to small imprecision in bearing (see text page 47).

Only Apparently Steady Bearing

The following are examples of particular dangers when navigating by radar with a VSR (very short range) setting.

A careless observer who sets the bearing line onto a new contact and does not check up on this until 15 minutes later could deduce that a bearing is steady when in fact it is not, and could initiate a collision-avoidance manoeuvre leading to difficulties.

Fig.26 shows a contact which on $K_1 \to K_2$ would have crossed our bows. However, K thought about this and considered it safer, unnoticed by our observer, to alter course to starboard to pass astern of us. The second time he looks, our observer sees him at K_3, and possibly he stops just as K has resumed his old course. (According to the rules we should have maintained a steady course and speed, but it is precisely those who are careless and unprepared who tend to take panic action.)

Fig. 27 shows another reason why in fog, we may decide a bearing is steady when it is not. We (e) are in a motor yacht. K, having no radar, hears us loud and clear but is uncertain about the location of the noise source, as is often the case in fog. For that reason he stops at 2 and so, due to our inattention and speed, turns up at K_3 on the PPI. The emergency turn to starboard apparently called for because of our sloppy observation could well result in our ramming K.

Fig. 26

Fig. 27

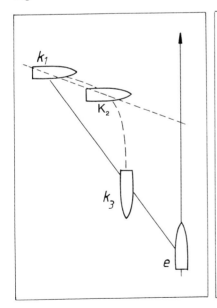
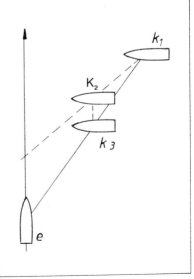

Bearing Not Steady — Collision

Fig.28 shows a situation which in narrow estuarial waters and with the radar on VSR can quickly become dangerous. Contact K shows up only when we are already very close to him. He has been lying stopped, perhaps because he has heard a fog signal which has escaped us because of our own engine noise. We saw someone pass to port on the PPI. Our skipper has switched off the automatic fog signal because the continuous hooting gets on his nerves – he's got radar, after all.

K, who does not have radar, gets under way because he neither sees nor hears us and the vessel duly hooting is audibly getting further away. Just because the bearing is changing is no excuse for us to relax; because the VSR setting has allowed all this to develop too close to us, we are in danger.

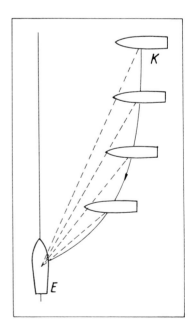

Fig. 28   Collision although bearing has not remained steady (see text above).

Encounter at an Acute Angle

Fig.29 shows a sequence of events leading to a 'radar-assisted collision', something which has been written about many times and in the early days of radar frequently occurred. The cause is inadequate radar-training, though even today the possibility of something similar happening cannot be excluded.

Both vessels are here sailing at the same speed (which is not essential) but not on opposite courses as we (E) believe after the first radar contacts, particularly since at the time of the second plotting E was additionally 5° off course. It could be that K is on an acute-angle collision course with us, so we give the helm order 'ten degrees more'. That brings the pip, 6 nm away, once more 1 nm to port of our heading line but we slowly turn yet another 10° to increase the lateral distance some more — which, however, does not achieve much (position 4). So we turn even further to starboard, very shortly have to go 'hard over' and order a crash stop. Suddenly K appears broadside-on and dead ahead out of the fog; tries an emergency turn to port, but it takes far too long to get the vessel to start to turn. Result: crunch!

The radar picture that K observed, whilst keeping a steady course until the last minute, was that E was running towards him in a slight arc, but presumably he concentrated on bearings and these continued to open: at 10 nm 015°, at 4 nm 021°. (What's that nice little ditty again, for open-sea encounters? 'Green to green or red to red, perfect safety — go ahead.') Only at 1 nm target separation does the lateral distance from the heading line get a bit too tight for K, which he reckons to put right with a 5° turn to port — hereby depriving himself of the last chance of avoiding a collision.

Our bearing from K showed E all the time fine on the starboard bow, so he should really not have maintained his course. But then we did aggravate his problem by our minimal course alterations. And both those with the con had that fatal 'green to green' buzzing away at the back of their minds: it has no validity for radar. And we also would have been rebuked by the marine court, that we did not pay enough attention to a contact fine on the port bow.

Furthermore: '... successive small alterations of course and/or speed should be avoided.' (Rule 8b, International Regulations for the Prevention of Collisions at Sea. IRPCS). Should? Must!

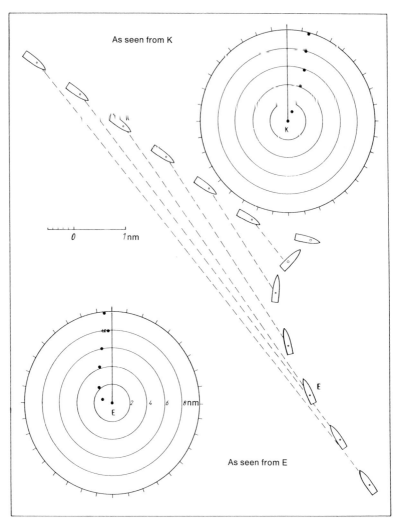

Fig. 29   'Radar-assisted' collision (see text page 51).

Course Alterations

According to rule 8 of the above regulations, alterations of course or speed should be positive, timely, and large enough for another vessel to recognise them quickly, visually or by radar. Because of the considerable differences in the speed of vessels, and even more because of the enormous differences in their bulk, in dense traffic at sea it is scarcely possible to give a sufficiently early and clear indication of what one is doing.

Anyone in a slow craft is advised to make course alterations of 90° to make clear also to the radar observer in the large and fast vessel how positive they are. After all, our pip is creeping across the big fellow's PPI with all the speed of a moribund mite. 'Never alter course by less than 60°' applies even to fast motor yachts.

Fig.30 shows an exact construction of the developing situation if a 4.2-knot yacht starts a 90° turn to avoid a fast vessel (a) heading for it at 21 knots when they are already only 1 nm apart — imagine, or draw on a larger scale, what would happen if it had only altered course by 45°. In a second situation it encounters a coaster (b) steaming at 9 knots and immediately turns away 90° to starboard. That is a bit more comfortable; the minimum distance apart is 4 cables (= 0.4 nm). In the case of a rather slower freighter, less than 3 min. is all the time you have to get yourself out of danger even with a 90° turn.

Slowing Down, Stopping

According to rule 8 of the IRPCS, speed alterations also should be so obvious that they are quickly recognisable on the PPI. Let us see in Fig.31 how the speed alteration of K, who has to get out of our way, looks on the chart and on our PPI. We are steaming at 18 knots and have set the radar range to 12 nm. At 12 nm we make contact with K on a relative bearing of 326°; 10 minutes later K bears 329° at 8.2 nm — he is closing at 22.8 knots, so he is a fast one too. (Attention, please — relative-speed trap!) If he carries on going as he has been on the PPI, he will cross our bows at a distance of 2 nm. But K obviously also has radar, and crossing our

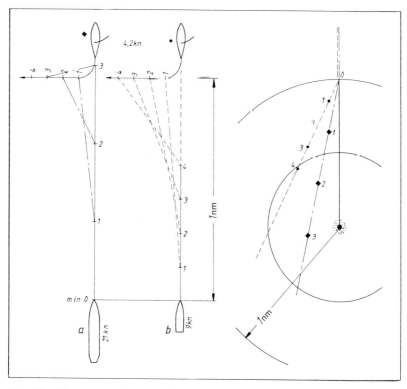

Fig. 30   Representation of emergency turns on the radar screen
(see text page 53).

bows seems to look too dangerous to him. Having recognised, 10 min. after making contact with us, that things could get tricky, he cuts his speed down by half — by no means too soon or too much, as we shall see. The kink in his trace on the PPI shows that his absolutely positive action was only just adequate. K had the option of stopping altogether later, but that would have taken longer and accelerating again from stopped would have required more energy. And altering course to pass astern of us would also have been less economical; try plotting it, if you like.

    Looking at the vector diagram on the left alongside the radar plot in Fig.31, was it clear to you that the contact's initial speed was 14.4 knots, and how together with an own speed of 18 knots

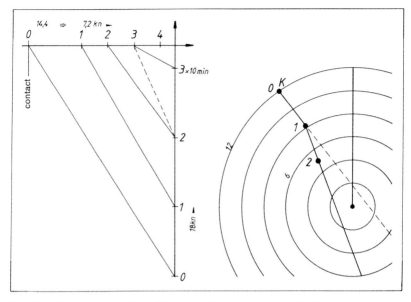

Fig. 31   The contact alters his speed (see text page 53–4).

that can add up on the PPI (vectorially) to a closing speed of 22.8 knots?

Finally, it is necessary to draw attention to rule 19d of the IRPCS, 'conduct of vessels in restricted visibility', which for location of another vessel by radar calls for a check on whether a close-quarters situation is developing and/or there is a risk of collision. If it is decided to alter course, this alteration should not, except when overtaking, be made to port if the vessel bears forward of the beam, nor towards a vessel on or aft of the beam.

Pre-drawn Relative Motion Plots
In some of the preceding drawings, we plotted on a complete circle and pre-drawn distance rings. The technical term for that sort of proforma is 'relative motion plot'. In earlier days, when the majority of vessels and navies were using simple radar sets you could buy printed copies. But nowadays professional navigators use sophisticated sets that compute the answers and these printed plotting sheets are hard to find.

Manoeuvring Geometry

This chapter concerns what has to be done if we, as the give-way boat, have to carry out a manoeuvre to avoid a close-quarters situation, or even indeed a collision.

The legal requirements are stated in rules 2, 5, 6 and 19 of the IRPCS, which every skipper or watchkeeper at sea must know and have handy in print on board.

What are 'Close Quarters'?

To ask the question more accurately: what are close quarters for a fishing boat or a yacht? After all, these are nimble craft, stoppable within a few metres.

That is the way big-ship captains think, whose conception of close quarters is shaped by dislike of course-altering turns and rapid stops. Small-craft skippers think entirely differently: their vessel is small and easily overlooked, often slow, and has a lot of trouble in reaching a safe distance from a fast ship, which also involves taking into account the height and steepness of the fast ship's bow wave. We have read already that if using radar, the 1-nm ring on the PPI can be too close for comfort.

Plotting Tools

In order to make quick decisions, we need some simple tools with which to work directly on the PPI.

Notched Rulers
We need something with which we can, quickly and without maths, apply a time-scale for our own speed to the PPI. These are very simple instruments which for immediate needs can be made from cardboard, paper, or more lastingly from transparent or coloured plastic which can be designed to follow the curvature of the PPI. A DIY type of tool.

You need several notched rulers:
1. One each for normal cruising speed in (a) good and (b) bad weather, (c) for speed at night and in fog.
2. One each for (a) the long observation range of 8–12 nm, and (b) for the shorter range of 4–8 nm when near the coast.

The scale for the respective ranges is most easily obtained with the radar on and switched to the appropriate range, from the spacing of the distance rings which, as with typewriters and computers, is still based on inches. 25.4 mm = 1 inch for x nm is probably the basis for the spacing of the PPI distance rings in all small radars.

The notches in the rulers are best made at 6-min. intervals; i.e. tenths of hours, which makes mental arithmetic easy. Assuming 1 inch space between rings corresponds to 2 nm, and our cruising speed in good weather is 22 knots (i.e. 2.2 nm/6 min.) we calculate the notch spacing in metric terms as

$$\frac{25.4 \, \text{mm} \times 2.2 \, \text{nm}}{2 \, \text{nm}} = 27.94 \, \text{mm} \simeq 28 \, \text{mm}$$

Five notches should be enough, since they cover half an hour.

Writing Implements

Plotting on the PPI is done with a fine felt pen, with which you can also write on glass. Wet or dry, the ink can be wiped off with a paper handkerchief, even off acrylic (Plexi) glass. As the pelorus above sets with CRTs is often of acrylic glass, take care not to use felt pens that etch plastic foil, because their marks cannot be removed.

Stopwatch

It is surprising that radar sets do not as yet have one of these built in. Anyone with an LCD stopwatch has only himself to blame for night-time problems. The illumination, if any, is usually too feeble and often there is none at all. A pocket torch providing red light which does not upset night vision should be standard equipment for night passages in every vessel.

Plotter-equipped Sets

Certain sets show a light-trace with time-marks for contacts, but if you eliminate the trace(s) the whole picture disappears and then builds up again, which is tiresome. Other sets plot at 10-second intervals, but only eight or ten points, any astern of these being extinguished; in video technique, the substitute for afterglow.

Collision Avoidance Manoeuvres

Fig.32 shows how to use a notched ruler on the PPI or the relative motion plot, to construct a collision avoidance manoeuvre. Three plottings at 6-min. intervals show that contact K is closing on a collision course. Our decision is to make a turn when the contact has reached K_x, so that we pass at a minimum distance of 1.5 nm. Draw a tangent from K_x to the 1.5 nm ring in such a way that the contact cuts our heading line, because for contacts approaching from for'd of the beam and with the right of way, it is the quickest way of executing the manoeuvre.

We draw a parallel to this new track through K_3 and lay the notched ruler parallel to the heading line, with a notch at K_1. We then mark point e at the second notch below (corresponding to 12 min. travel), and rotate the ruler about this point until the original notch is on the parallel to the new track. If you now turn the

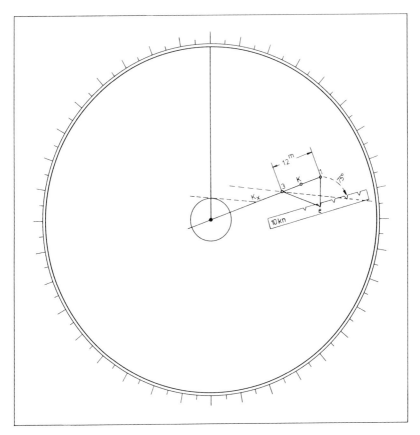

Fig. 32   How to use a notched ruler (see text page 58).

heading line parallel to the ruler, you can read off the magnitude of the necessary course alteration at time K_x — here $+ 75°$ — from the compass rose.

Because the contact is faster (e $\rightarrow$ 3), the ruler could also be turned anticlockwise, but that would reduce the closing rate too much and draw out the manoeuvre interminably. If your own ship is the faster (Fig.33), course can be altered to make the contact pass astern, but that is dangerous and takes longer because the closing speed v_a^1 is less than v_a.

Whether you prefer to work on the relative motion plot with

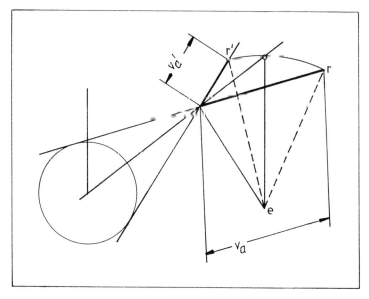

Fig. 33   Geometry for 'being the faster vessel, making the emergency turn to starboard or to port' (see text page 59).

compasses rather than with a notched ruler is a matter of taste. When working on the PPI use compasses with rubber points.

For acute-approach-angle encounter collision-avoidance manoeuvres, course alterations constructed in this way are not obvious enough.

The emergency turn should be given preference if there is enough room for it. It must not be used if it means cutting across the bows of another ship, or getting too close to a vessel on the beam steaming at the same speed. Then the only thing left to do is slow down — and in good time.

Slowing-down Manoeuvre

As Fig.34 shows, this is a very simple construction. Again we have a contact closing on a collision course, as we recognise after 6 min. of plotting, and we decide to slow down at once so that the contact passes us with a minimum distance of 2 nm. We draw the tangent from '6' to the 2-nm ring and extend it backwards to cut our own-speed vector e → r. The vector-portion cut off, e → r^1 = 0.55(e → r), indicates by how much we have to reduce speed; here to 55%. Reminder: the tangent is the new track of the contact as soon as we have slowed down.

Theoretically, speeding up is also an option, i.e. draw the tangent to the other side of the distance-ring and extend e → r upwards (acceleration) until it cuts the tangent; here our craft would need to be able to increase speed by 278.5%.

Fig.35 shows an arbitrary speed reduction of 70%. (e → r) = 100% and e is the starting point for our own-speed vector. It is important that you remember this. Maths buffs will immediately discover what they can do here with their pocket calculators.

Advice
Slowing down in time is more economical than stopping later. This has to do with the propeller's power consumption curve when accelerating, which is not a cubic parabola unless you increase power extremely slowly. Slowing down is probably in most cases more economical than making an emergency turn, but has the disadvantage that if you are navigating by radar in poor visibility it is less easy to recognise on the PPI. Avoid simultaneous alterations of course and speed (other than as a last resort).

Rules for Manoeuvring

What is discussed in this chapter can be summed up in a few mnemonic rules. We always base our manoeuvre on the direction and speed of the traces of our contacts, best recognised on a PPI with a long afterglow, or on video-PPIs by appropriate plot signs (tails). Yachts 20 m (65 ft) long or longer ought to be fitted with north-stabilisable radar, which nowadays no longer requires a gyro-compass; fluxgate plus computer will do equally well, which makes the deal a whole lot cheaper.

We must establish the following: every contact on the PPI moving parallel/at an angle to the heading line in the same direc-

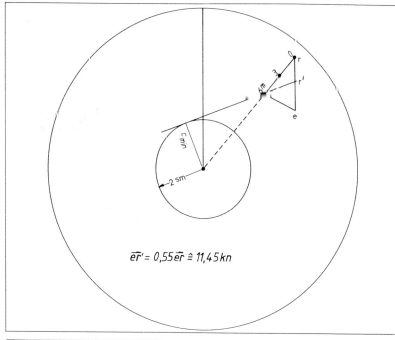

$$\overline{er'} = 0,55\,\overline{er} \cong 11,45\,kn$$

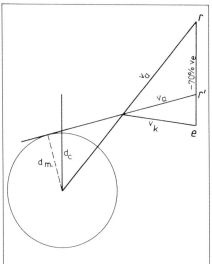

Fig. 34 (above) Geometry for 'collision avoidance by speed reduction'.

Fig. 35 (left) Speed reduction by 70%. If the angle of intersection between contact track and heading line is not too acute, it is more practical to use d_c instead of d_{min} because it simplifies the calculation.

tion displaces upwards. Every contact with a declivity in the opposite direction to the heading line displaces downwards. A trace lying at right angles to the heading line is running athwart.

Mnemonic Rule 1
In whichever PPI-quadrant it may be located, every contact displacing upwards gets a kink to the left in its trace if your own ship turns right (the opposite if your own ship turns left).

Mnemonic Rule 2
In whichever PPI-quadrant it may be located, every contact displacing downwards gets a kink to the right in its trace if your ship turns right (the opposite if the your ship turns left).

Mnemonic Rule 3
If one's own ship slows down or stops, the traces of all contacts get a kink upwards.

Mnemonic Rule 4
If one's own ship increases speed, all traces get a kink downwards.

Mnemonic Rule 5
Contacts with traces running upwards or athwart are faster than we are.

Mnemonic Rule 6
Where a contact's trace indicates high speed, the effect of your own ship's collision-avoidance manoeuvres is small and slow. If the contact's speed exceeds one's own maximum, he can only be outmanoeuvred with difficulty. (Run at right angles to his course at full speed to gain distance!)

Mnemonic Rule 7
If one's own speed exceeds the contact's, one is master of the situation.

Mnemonic Rule 8
A contact that does not make a trace restricts one's freedom of manoeuvre; he is on the same course, sailing at the same speed, as one's own ship.

Remember North-stabilised radars can have the heading line at any angle to the ship's centreline, even pointing backwards (southerly course), but it continues to determine what is upwards.

Navigation Using Radar

Almost all yachts that have a radar set use it for navigation, or rather more precisely, for pilotage. Whether you can see or not, with a radar set you can achieve almost everything that is possible by conventional terrestrial navigation, anything you can do with your eyes is possible by utilising the high-frequency electromagnetic waves of the radar set, which are almost the same as light. There is one operation, however, which the seafarer cannot carry out with radar: that is to measure the vertical sextant angle of objects and from these calculate his distance from them.

Navigation using radar consists almost entirely of taking bearings and ranges from and to landmarks and fixed sea marks, the range generally being more accurate than the bearing.

In radar literature there have been those who favour the 3-range position-finding system similar to the 'cocked hat' from RDF bearings or three star sights. This idea is somewhat impractical, because if the length of one bearing line were to be measured wrongly then so, also, would the others. Also, with the relatively small distances for precise position-finding (in practice little greater than the range of vision) it is all too rare for the objects providing the bearings to form a triangle.

The bearing line (relative bearing) is our line of position, and the generally available variable distance ring bisects it with a fair degree of accuracy.

Interpreting the Picture

Because the radar beam is lobe shaped (Fig.36), capes, jetties, small islands and similarly shaped bits of land are shown on the PPI wider than they would be to scale. This does not necessarily make a bearing imprecise if you work from the centre of the widened contour, but unfortunately that centre is not always the

Fig. 36 Spreading of the coast contours as a result of the lobe-shape of the radar beam.

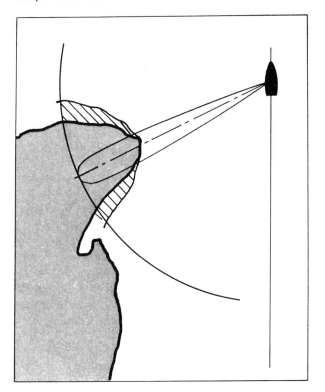

right place. If the boat in Fig.36 were to be transmitting from 5 cm. further 'south', the north side of the cape would be masked, not visible to the radar and thus not shown on the PPI. So one usually has to arrive at an understanding of what one is seeing on the PPI, and that often is not possible without a 1:150 000, or larger, scale chart.

The requirement for enlarged representation, say 1:20 000, is often already met on such charts by insets. Sticking out from the cape in Fig.36 there could additionally be a flat spit not recognised by the radar. A similar situation arises with the sandy beaches of the East Frisian islands, which at low water springs are very wide and flat; the coastline then shown on the PPI is not the beach/water boundary but rather the chain of dunes. A tower on such a beach can look on the PPI like a ship anchored there, because the beach does not show. Mud flats do not show up well either.

Marshes, shifting dunes and gentle mounds may provide only a faint echo; woods and habitations on gently rising terrain produce a very broad background echo, as do villages.

Low atolls with a reasonably thick growth of palms usually show up well on the PPI, because the surface of the water and the tree-growth face combine to act as an amplifying corner reflector. Lagoons are not shown because the usually smooth water behind the isthmus or sand bar reflects the radar beam away from the source. The reef of an atoll shows up best at low water, when it has dried; at high water it is best recognisable by the echo from the surf. However, on the PPI that will appear as a gently floating veil-like strip which does not catch the observer's eye. The entrance through such an annular reef will be recognisable on the PPI only when you are radially outside it, otherwise the masking effect will keep it hidden.

Chart and PPI

The difference between chart and PPI is the 'masking' effect. The chart-maker has looked at the area from high up; the radar scanner is looking from a height of only a few metres. The PPI may, for example, from outside St Peter Port on Guernsey show a view of the harbour indicating it to be empty of other yachts. Don't you believe it! As usual it is bulging with yachts, but the radar cannot see what is behind the high moles. If you are comparing chart and PPI, always remember that your radar scanner throws a beam with long shadows, like the low sun (see Figs 37, 38).

The electronic chart has been invented, stored on digital discs which are scarcely any more expensive than charts on paper. Corrections are also supplied on laser discs. The only snag is that the equipment for turning this digital information into a chart on the viewing-screen is bulky and costly, more the sort of thing for mega-yachts. Electronic equipment may be interconnected, so also can the electronic chart with radar and radio location processes. Impractical for most small-craft skippers, but who knows? After all, powerful computers are getting smaller and cheaper.

External Navigational Aids, Radar Beacons

'Racons' are important navigational markers which when struck by a radar beam emit an identification signal tuned to our radar frequency, which is depicted as a line or a Morse signal. In the case of Kiel lighthouse, for instance, once you are within a certain range – · – (kilo) appears on the PPI at more or less regular intervals, depending on the seaway, pointing towards the PPI centre and whose end nearest that centre indicates the position of the lighthouse. (It is always the case that the end of the paint nearest the PPI centre indicates the position of the racon, as regards both bearing and distance. On the charts, navigational aids with that capability are labelled 'Racon'.)

'Ramark' indicates a nowadays rare bearing-only radar beacon which transmits continuously, not only on demand.

In a photo-chart comparison in Fig.45 the Racon-markings of buoy H2 are shown close to the craft, in the Hubertgat; those of the Westerems buoy on a relative bearing of 305° off the entry to the Randzelgat to the west of Borkum. Both indicate the navigable mouths of the Ems but do not have any special characteristic — unnecessary in most cases because even Sunday skippers incapable of navigating have some idea of where they are.

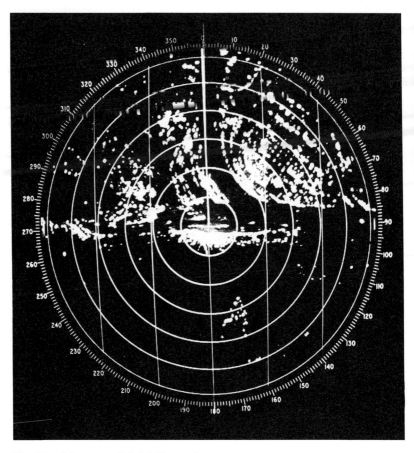

Fig. 37 (above and right) The radar scanner is on top of the harbour office. Range setting 1.5 nm; ring spacing 0.25 nm.

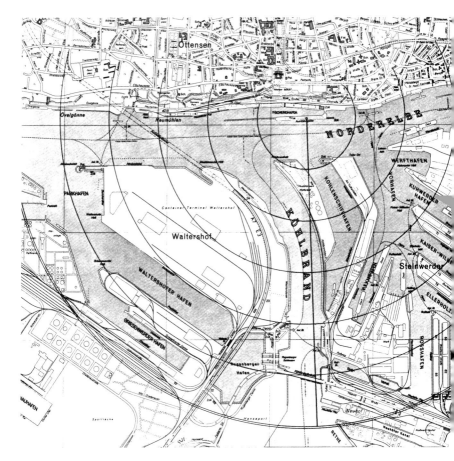

Some Warnings and Reservations

Because of the increasing number of Racons, many charts no longer show their identification characteristics alongside the marks. They are, however, included in the List of Lights. The actual range of the aid is 50–100 m (164–328 ft) less than the mark indicates. The Racon frequency shifts over a range of 3300–3500 MHz in the space, usually, of a minute.

The point in time when the signal becomes recognisable depends on the height of your scanner and of the Racon aerial, and on the respective transmitter powers. Figures given in the lists are

69

Fig. 38   (above and right) Range setting 6 nm, ring spacing 1 nm.
The RH long mark astern is Kiel lighthouse, the other is a large
vessel. The picture shows so many small craft that it is barely
possible to identify the buoys. Note that the radar cannot 'see'
around the corners of Bülk Head and Nienhof Head; it sees only the
entrance to Kiel Fjord between Bülk and Laboe. The heading line
shows 272°. The radar picture here has not been turned parallel to
the chart but instead shows how the radar-watcher has to cope with
screen and chart.

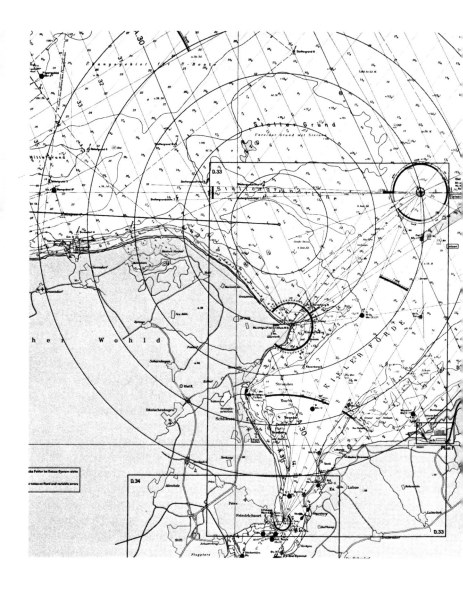

only approximate. Racon signals can overshoot; you must not trust a signal which, according to dead reckoning or some other method, cannot yet be visible.

Racon signals can interfere badly with close-quarters observations; if that is so, they can usually be suppressed, or attenuated sufficiently, with anti clutter rain. Racons may be temporarily out of commission for maintenance, without any special notification.

Objects Behind the Horizon and Landfall

Fig.39 explains an effect which can sometimes be observed, which can make the radar operator believe land is advancing toward him. The situation represents an island or a steep-to coastline.

Fig. 39 Land on the move. On the radar screen, the land seems to be advancing towards the ship.

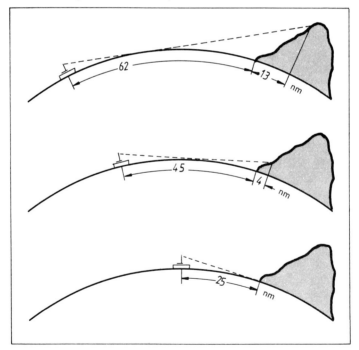

Radar Fixes

Bearings

Because of the width of the radar beam these are not very accurate. But on small (up to 40 m (130 ft) long) vessels in a seaway they are more accurate than a visual bearing using a pelorus or a hand-bearing compass with unknown errors.

Range and Bearing

You are unlikely to take cross bearings, but rounding a cape by keeping at a predetermined distance from it is easy by keeping it on the beam until it bears 15° abaft, staying on this course, then changing course again until it is on the beam, and so on. This is a proper, and with radar a particularly simple, procedure, especially since it also gives you continual control over the range. Even the major cornerstones of world navigation, such as Ushant, Finisterre, St Vincent, etc., can be rounded in this way.

The smaller the object, the more accurate its radar bearing, but in the case of buoys you must always bear in mind that they may have drifted and that radar cannot identify which buoy it is scanning (Racon excepted). Incidentally, in a rain shower buoys can disappear from the PPI as well as from sight.

A big help when navigating by radar is that since 1982 fairway buoys have been laid in pairs. (See the radar photos of the Randzel deep, Fig.52)

There is no objection to crossing a visual bearing with a radar one, which can be useful in the case of lighthouses partway down the slope of a bluff and thus not showing on the PPI. In the case of larger islands, you can take tangential bearings some distance apart (Fig.40). Because of the width of the radar beam, the intersection of the two bearing lines is too close to the island, but then the radar anyway gives you the distance from the middle of the island.

Two or more Ranges

Distances measured by radar are more accurate than bearings. If the set has not got a variable range marker, you use the previously described notched ruler between the fixed range on the PPI to get a more accurate range. Apart from that, you need a compass with a

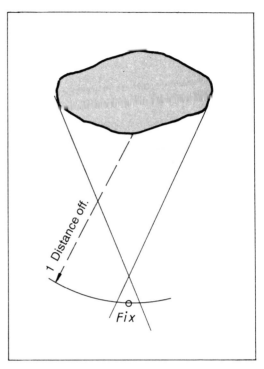

Fig. 40   Tangent bearing and range.

pencil point, to draw the respective range arcs on the chart (Fig.41).

Difficulties
When making a landfall on a coast with few distinctive features, or indeed one with too many such as the Skerries, it is often difficult even with radar to know where you are. What you can do is to take a few bearings and ranges, plot them on transparent paper and by sliding this about try to reconcile plot and chart. If you can get a rough fix this way, you will usually have more success in interpreting the PPI. In the case of a coast with low, flat-surface beaches, there can be very considerable uncertainty about the actual coast-

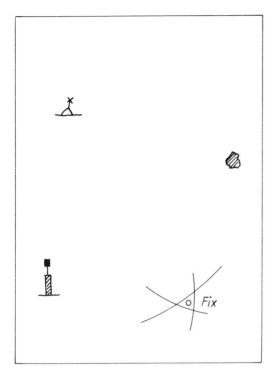

Fig. 41   Fix from three radar ranges.

line. The only help then is comparison with the chart: where are there houses? Where are edges of woods, lines of dune shown, which probably would be visible on the PPI? Off steep coastlines, with the usual barely 60 cm (2 ft) long yacht scanner, it is very difficult to discern a harbour entrance from three or four miles out. Particularly in the Mediterranean, where, because of the high humidity of the air there is often a haze covering the coast, it can happen that you do not know whether to steer to the right or to the left to find the harbour. (This is just to give you an indication that radar does not release you from the routine work of navigation.)

Running along a monotonous coast it is often impossible to obtain a fix by means of bearing and range or two range circles, but a continuous control of the range combined with the little extra effort of a precise dead reckoning on the chart is usually enough to keep you safe.

Experience in making observations in often-visited narrow and difficult estuarial waters in good weather can be invaluable if at some time one has to pass through when the visibility is poor, particularly if during the good weather the navigator notes those good radar aspects which in bad weather help towards a safe transit.

Ghost echoes can occur and are usually very fast and manoeuvrable. Like mirages, they are based on differences of density within the air mass which disturb the latter's conductivity. Both often occur together.

Radar alone is never sufficient for safe navigation, and wishful thinking is particularly dangerous when navigating by radar.

Fig. 42   Passing clearance p, relative bearing σ and range d.

Running Fixes Using Radar

A useful rule of thumb (Fig.42):

$$\text{Passing clearance} = \frac{\text{Relative bearing} \times \text{distance}}{60}$$

and arranged differently:

$$\text{Relative bearing} = \frac{60 \times \text{Passing clearance}}{\text{Distance}}$$

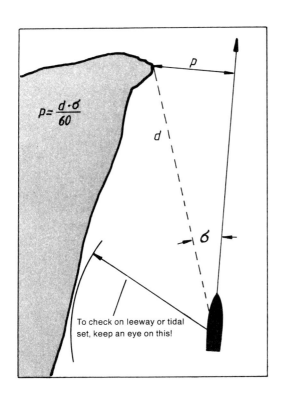

$$p = \frac{d \cdot \sigma}{60}$$

To check on leeway or tidal set, keep an eye on this!

This rule of thumb becomes accurate if you replace the figure 60 by 57.296 (the radians unit). Even so, because of the width of the radar beam it is accurate enough for practical purposes, but not what one would call precise. In the rearranged form, the rule is used, for instance, in order to calculate how to give a buoy to be passed a desired clearance in an athwartships-drift situation. If you turn the vessel so that the calculated relative bearing is on the pip of the buoy, you can read off from the compass what course to steer. Of course the relative bearing increases as you approach the buoy, but the compass course, once established, embodies the necessary aim-off.

Fig. 43   Parallel graticule for identification of set towards the land – eg if the coast contour touching the second line 'wanders' to the left across this.

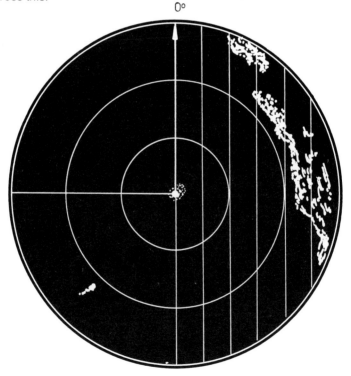

Usefulness of the Pelorus

The modern digital video radars mostly have a bearing line which can be superimposed and rotated electronically, but no longer a transparent pelorus rotatable above the PPI as the worthy CRT sets used to have. Figs 43 and 44 show how this pelorus usually looked, and give examples of what one could do with it. If one of the parallel lines started as a tangent to a headland, and that headland then wandered 'inwards' across it, it did not need any deliberation to be certain that one was being set shorewards. If you marked the pip of a buoy a few times with a grease pencil and rotated the grid parallel to the line of those plots, this gave you the angle of drift of

Fig. 44   Angle or drift (leeway or tidal set) deduced from plotting a buoy three times.

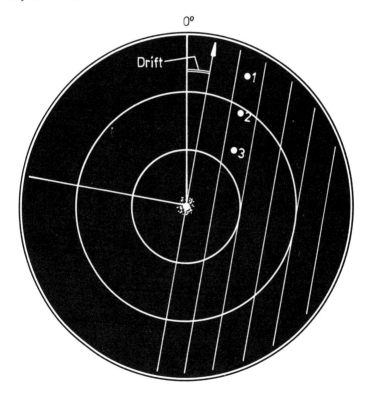

your yacht very accurately, since the heading line indicates the line of your keel. Speed over the ground derives from the distance between '1' and '3' scaled as appropriate. Buoys 'on an opposite course' on the PPI are splendid speedometers.

Estuary and River Sailing

The radars designed for small-craft skippers — and that includes fishing boats — are entirely suitable for navigating in poor visibility in the estuaries of big rivers such as the Thames, Clyde, Elbe, Rhine and Hudson, so long as they satisfy the basic requirements stated right at the beginning. Aerial length at least 60 cm (2 ft), pulse length compatible with good distant resolution and clearly 'painting' VDU. The recent practice of laying fairway buoys in pairs has greatly simplified estuarial navigation by radar. The only surprise for the unwary might be HT-cables crossing above the river, which have the appearance on the PPI of a small boat leaving the shore and crossing before you. A higher degree of sophistication is required of a commercial river-radar, and the sets cost more.

There is no objection whatever to a yacht using its radar on a river like the Rhine, but only in good visibility. In fog it may not proceed on many major waterways despite its radar, because a small radar will not be good enough to separate the echoes of the radar reflectors mounted on the bridge piers, or on buoys only a few metres ahead of them, from those of the bridge itself lying like a barricade across the river, and so therefore identify a safe passage through on the PPI.

Radar provides a means for fixing the ship and steering it into safe waters when visibility is poor, or for keeping it a safe distance from the shore when there are no other means available.

Since range is more accurate than bearing, two range determinations are better than two bearings or bearing and range of a marker. However, certainty about what is creating the echoes is obtained only infrequently in practice. Wherever the opportunity of taking a visual bearing exists, one should seize it.

Processing a Relative Bearing

Our head-up non-stabilised radar produces only relative bearings reading from 000 clockwise to 360. The figure for everything to port is greater than 180, and that is not a bad thing because it means we do not have to remember any rules about signs.

At the time of taking the radar bearing, we must also read the compass, apply the deviation, if any, and the appropriate sign to that compass course to correct it, add the radar bearing to it, and finally correct this sum by applying the variation with its correct sign. That gives the true bearing which we can draw on the chart; if it turns out to be a bit too big, we have to subtract 360.

Since we are correcting, all corrections keep their proper sign; i.e. minus for port deviation and west variation. For example:

> Radar bearing 083
> Compass course 333 +
> Deviation 004 +
> Variation 009 −
> True bearing 411
> Subtraction 360 −
> True bearing 051

It is certainly not my intention to tread on the sensitive corns of seasoned navigators with this advice, but after all there are also a lot of Sunday skippers who habitually navigate by stretches of coast they know — water towers and lighthouses, flagstaffs and the masts of museum ships, or a Hotel Bella Vista — all features that do not show up in the radar picture because that only gives a pretty crude simplified version of the known, or unknown, environs. Piers, quays and moles are usually easily recognisable, but a landing stage can look like a projection from a building.

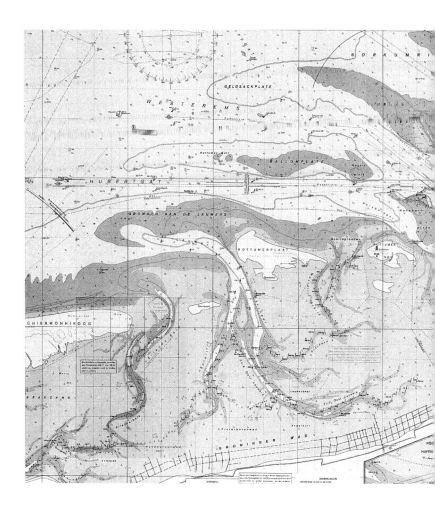

We are entering the mouth of the Ems using radar

To finish with, I will let Gert Büttgenbach in his motor yacht
Simulator enter the mouth of the Ems coming from the west, in fog,
to demonstrate the most useful aspects of radar for navigation, and
what most skippers will find of greatest assistance. The run has
been simulated using a computer, for that is the sort of programme
Büttgenbach understands. I expect in practice it would go just as

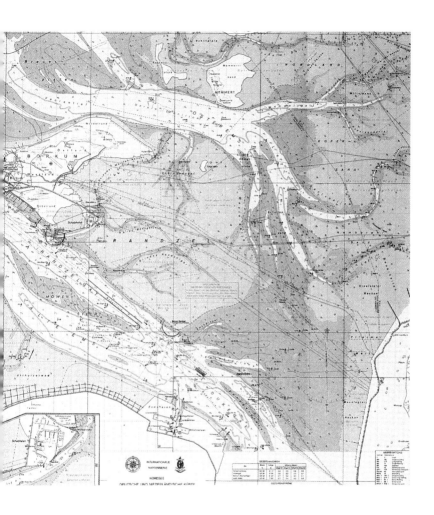

smoothly, but it would not be so simple to photograph. It could happen that the sunlight fell on to the VDU, or the tripod could fall over at a critical moment.

However, I can assure those of my readers who have never yet used radar for navigation that provided you have the right radar correctly adjusted, it is just as easy in real life since the fairway buoys have been laid in pairs.

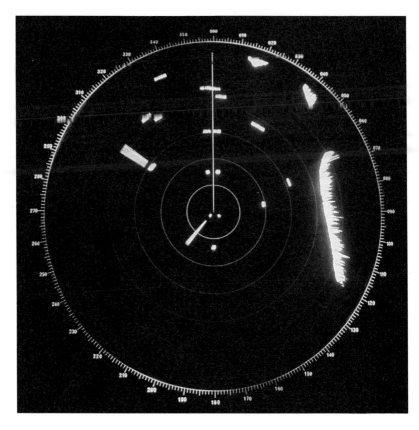

Fig. 45 Mouth of the Ems: the vessel, steering 090T, is at the outer end of the Hubertgat fairway. The port buoy (H2) has a Racon, the landfall buoy is dead astern. The Racon buoy bearing 304 relative is the landfall for the Westerems fairway of which buoys 1, 2 and 3 are visible. The land to starboard, 4 nm off, is the Schiermonnikoog Oosterstrand. The pip to starboard on the 2 nm ring is a spherical buoy; that near the 3 nm ring is called Regulus. The trace bearing 030 relative marks the buoys L1/L2 of the Lauwers secondary fairway, smeared into one by the radar lobe.

The heading line runs precisely between the paired fairway buoys.
You can see that the pair 3 nm away is already almost smeared into
one. The angle tangent here is about 3 mm/33 mm = 0.091 rad,
which corresponds to a lobe angle of 5.21° – a simple yacht radar.

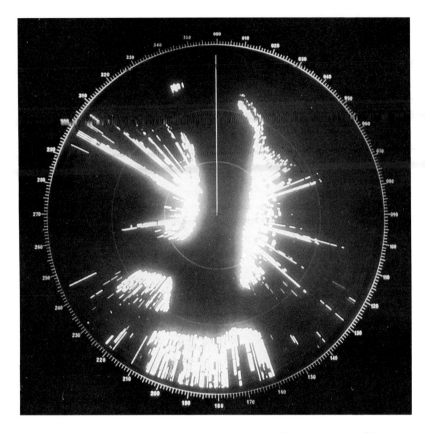

Figs. 46–47   Eemshaven: 1 We are sailing from Eemshaven on the
Dutch side of the mouth of the Ems. Of the LH mole, only the
extreme end shows, the other being in the radar-shadow of
buildings along the North Quay.

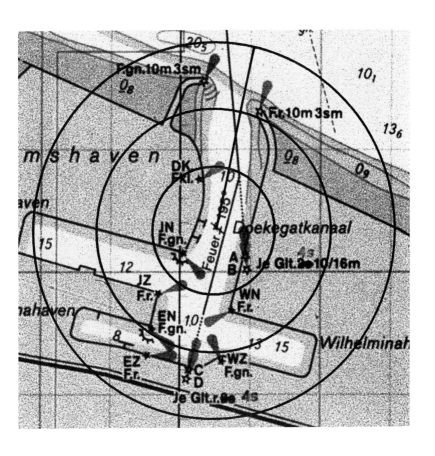

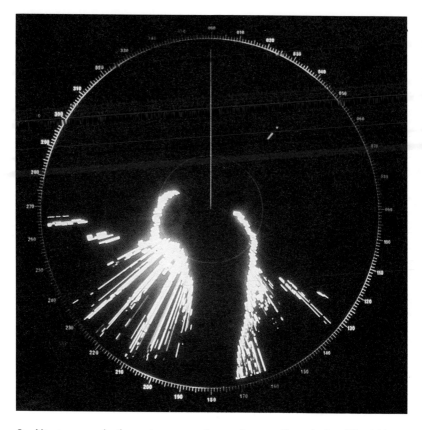

2 Now we are in the entrance and can also see the whole of the LH mole. Bearing 040, conical buoy 'Alte Ems 11'.

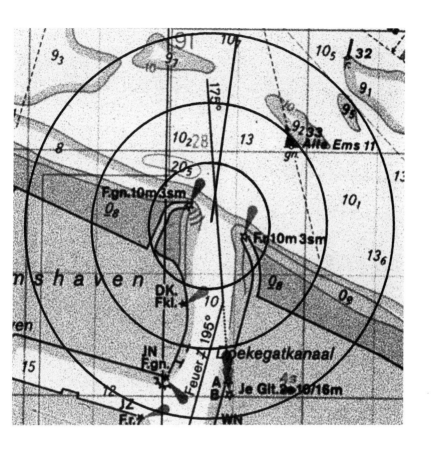

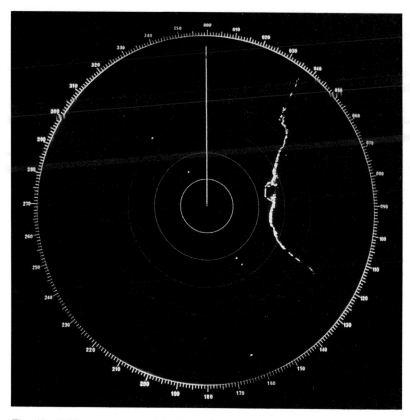

Fig. 48   With the range set for long distance, we are passing a
stretch of coast with an artificial harbour, bearing 075 relative;
display stabilised head-up.

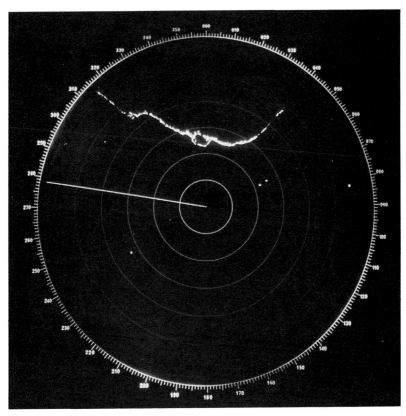

Fig. 49   This is what things look like with the display stabilised north-up. Our course is 278.

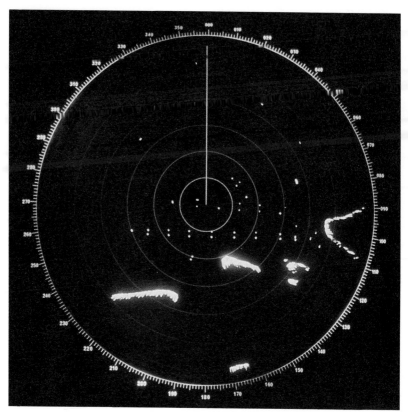

Fig. 50   West of Borkum in the Westerems fairway, radar north-up.
Range setting 12 nm. Of the next pair of buoys towards Borkum, only
the green is showing; the spar of the red is too thin. The land masses
in succession from W to E: Schiermonnikoog, Rottumerplaat,
Rottumeroog, Borkum, and near the southern edge a corner of the
Netherlands.

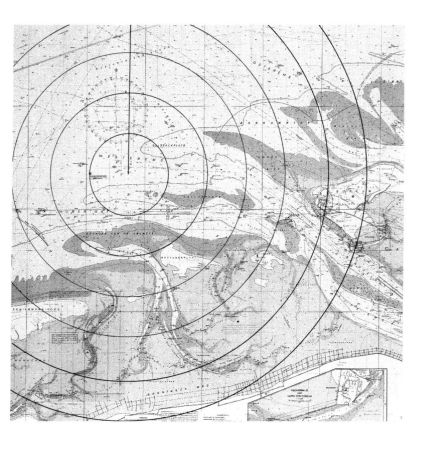

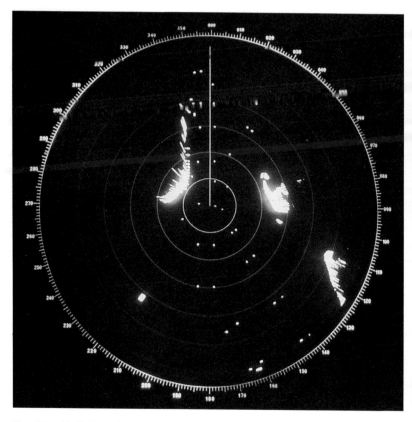

Fig. 51 (1–3) Entering the Ems; direction of travel upwards:
(1) To port the West Hook of Borkum. We are at the junction of the
Westerems and Hubertgat fairways, near the small Borkum
lighthouse. Bearing 220 there is a ship.

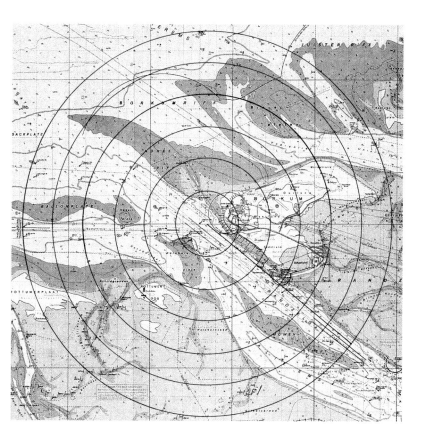

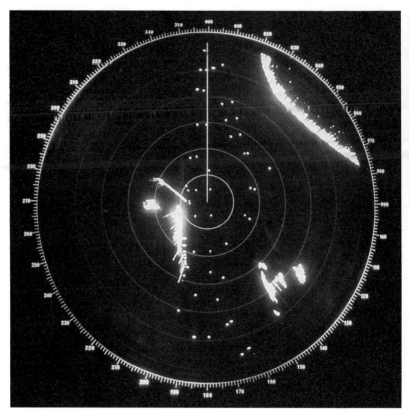

2   Now we are off the end of the leading dam for Borkum harbour. It is not high water, for then it would not be visible. At 020–075 the Dutch mainland is visible.

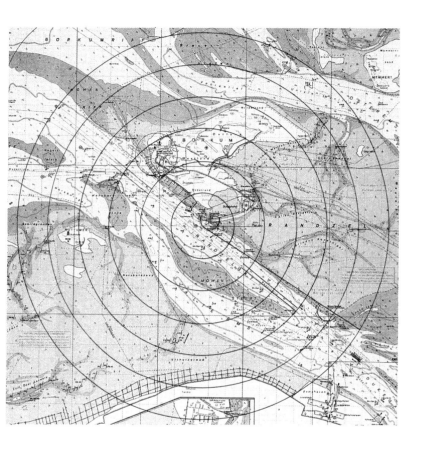

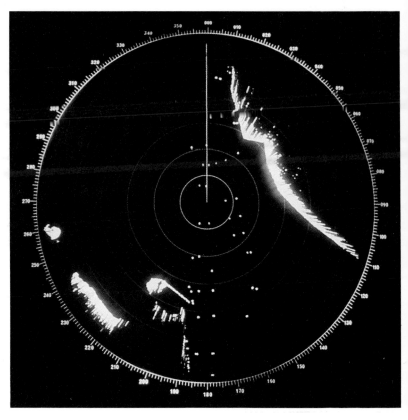

3   We are between the buoy-pairs 23/22 and 25/24 in the Randzelgat. On the mainland you can see the projecting corner of the artificially constructed Eemshaven and its entrance, further to the SE.

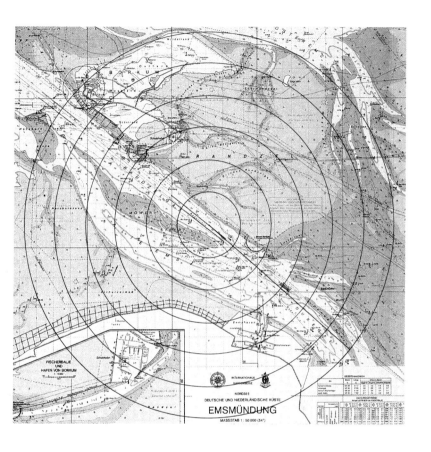

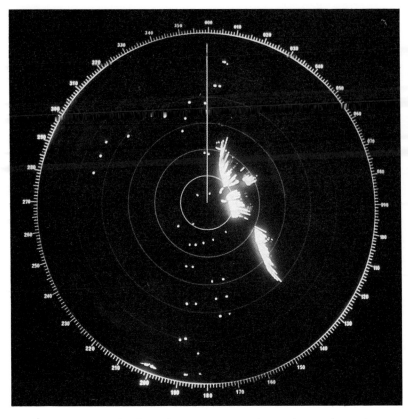

Fig. 52   We are off the Eemshaven entrance, have changed over to long range and are sailing up on the Ems to Leer.

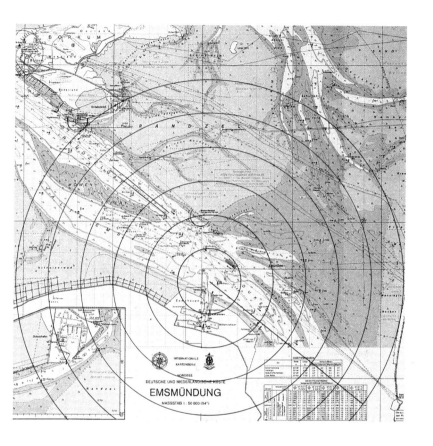

Some Radar Physics

Do not worry, nothing in this chapter falls outside the range of what is reasonably easy to understand. The intention is not that you should learn how to construct or repair a radar set, just that you should get to understand some of the technical data.

Measurement Using Radio Waves

Originally, in the mid–30s, a radar set was called a Radio Detection and Ranging set, from which the term 'radar' was derived. 'Radio' is now wrong, because the technology has moved away from that. Sparkover generates a spectrum of electromagnetic waves, such as can be heard as crackling from a radio receiver tuned to long or medium wave, with each lightning-strike during a thunderstorm. Radio technology started with something like that, but neither speech nor music could be transmitted that way, so 'radio broadcasting' is incorrect too.

Radio waves are an electromagnetic oscillation which diffuses through space approximately at the speed of light, spherically from a simple rod aerial. But just as you can focus light in a certain direction with parabolic mirrors, or let it radiate in only one direction through narrow slots, so you can also treat radio waves. However, these are not as easy to generate as light waves, just by means of a filament in a bulb. But you may be aware that light can be transmitted along a glass rod even if this is bent, the light being always totally reflected inwards when it strikes the walls of the rod, and conducted onwards. In much the same way the wave generated by the radar transmitter is conducted along a hollow waveguide — a copper tube usually rectangular in section — to the scanner. If the energy generated by the transmitter were sent to the scanner along a wire, like that from the maritime radio transmitter, that wire would already radiate energy like a non-directional aerial, and the radar's directional scanner would be short by that amount.

In the parabolic scanner the end of the waveguide is arranged with its aperture at the focal point of the mirror; in navigational radars with a rotating scanner, always angled downwards a bit to minimise the screening of the echoes received by the same scanner. In the slot scanner, the end length of the waveguide is rotatable about a vertical axis and has a number of narrow slots in one narrow-side wall, for the radiating energy to exit. The longer a slot scanner is, the better it focuses. Parabolic scanners nowadays mostly rotate inside a casing called a radome, to prevent their flying off in a gale. The slot scanner is preferred in the shipping business, because it does not produce any side lobes.

Radar sets can differ substantially in their technology, but in principle they are all the same. They send out a pulse, a pulse-modulated radio signal of extreme brevity and high power, and then switch the scanner over to the receiver for a comparatively lengthy period. Simultaneously the transmitter is sealed off from the scanner by a shut-off valve, to make quite sure no part of the very faint returning echoes of the emitted pulses is converted into useless heat in the transmitter. There must be a similar valve sealing off the receiver from the scanner during the transmitting period, to prevent the high input energy of the transmitted pulse destroying the sensitive receiver.

The pulse then rushes off with the speed of light $c = 300\,000$ km/s $\cong 162\,000$ nm/s; strikes an object which flings it back towards the scanner with the same speed. If we measure the time t between emission and return of the pulse, we can tell how far away the object is that created the echo. But because the time measured covers both the journey out and the journey back, we must take only half of it. Distance d equals speed × time, so d/nm = 162 000 nm/s × $(t/2)$s.

A radar pulse moves so fast that if it could follow the curvature of the earth it would travel around it at the equator 7.5 times in a single second. For that reason time in radar technology is usually (still) measured in millionth parts of a second, called microseconds (μs). That dates from the time when the only radars were ones with 10 cm (4 in) wavelengths (dm wave), whose short pulse duration was 1 μs. Modern small to medium-sized radars operate with wavelengths of 3 cm (1 in) with stronger pulses of 0.6–1 μs for long range, so a better time-unit would be the nanosecond (ns), 10^{-9}s or a billionth of a second; the briefer short-range pulse duration is 500 ns $\simeq$ 0.5 μs. A fresh pulse may only be emitted after the time for return to the outer limit of the range set has elapsed. The three parameters to consider for radars are carrier wave frequency (or wavelength), pulse duration and pulse repetition frequency.

Frequency

The higher the frequency, the shorter the wavelength, the smaller the objects that show up. Objects smaller than, roughly, the wavelength are overlooked by the wave. Using an analogy with water: a breakwater flings back the approaching waves and deflects some of the seaway around the head of the pier; a paving stone does neither the one nor the other.

But it is not all advantages with high frequency; it also shows up raindrops if there are a lot of them together; showers of rain, hail and snow appear as more or less dense light-patches, and a ship inside one of these shower areas may well be as invisible as the buoys usually are. Since 1977, a new technique of Decca's has been available whereby the peaks of such unwanted echoes are severely lopped, which at the same time makes the useful signals show up more clearly. A second video-processor which can additionally be switched in can amplify these yet again to double strength, see Fig. 6 to 12. The frequency of modern small radars lies in the region of 9–10 GHz (Gigahertz); Giga = 10^9.

Pulse Duration

The minimum distance measurable with a radar is determined by the pulse duration, because echoes from a short distance away which return while the transmitter is still emitting a pulse find that the receiver is deaf. Since the propagation velocity of radio waves is $c = 300$ m/µs, and only half the distance travelled in that microsecond is of interest, the shortest distance measurable with a pulse duration $t = 1$ µs is 150 m (500 ft). The same applies to resolution along the bearing line, i.e. with a pulse duration $t = 1$ µs, objects on the same bearing less than 150 m (500 ft). apart will be shown as one. As a general rule:

Resolution d m $= t$µs $\times$ 150 m/s. For instance:

Pulse duration	Resolution
µs	m
0.06	09.0
0.2	30.0
0.25	37.5
0.5	75.0

However, it is by no means the case that the shorter pulse duration is always the better, for this brevity also implies only a small amount of energy which even over a short distance of travel can be converted into heat and spread widely by attenuation and dispersion. For long distances you need long pulses, and the sets usually change that over as you turn the range knob. However, there are sets where you can switch to the long pulse even for short ranges, to show up targets reflecting only feebly.

Pulse Repetition Frequency

This is the number of pulses emitted per second; normally given as a figure/s ($=$ Hz) or as kilohertz (kHz). Pulse repetition frequency also is varied when the range is altered, since for long distances the pulse recurrence time (the reciprocal of pulse repetition frequency) of course needs to become longer.

The theoretical maximum range of a radar is:

$$d_{max} = \frac{80\,915 \text{ nm/s}}{\text{Pulse/s}}$$

(The explanation for the figure of 80 915 nm/s is that it is half of 161 830 nm/s, the precise speed of propagation of radio waves, and as has already been said only half interests us.)

Enough pulses have to be sent out to ensure that at least a proportion of them get back to be amplified, because after all the scanner is rotating so that its beam strikes any given object always only for a short time. If the scanner rotates at 15 rpm, a pulse repetition frequency of 800 Hz means that there are 8.89 pulses per degree of scanner rotation; generally

$$\frac{\text{No. of pulse/s} \times 60}{\text{revolutions/min} \times 360°}$$

The pulse repetition frequency additionally influences the mean transmitter power. Power is work (or energy) divided by time; nowadays standardised for electrical equipment and car or ship's engines as the Joule per second (J/s), called a watt, and 1000 watts are a kilowatt.

Peak Envelope Power
In that short pulse, considerable power is invested to make it go the full distance, since that is the sole push you can give it — rather like the power put into a football penalty kick. In the prospectuses, this power is designated 'peak envelope power', or alternatively 'pulse power'. The 3 kW they talk about there, would be sufficient to accelerate an 8 m (26 ft) seagoing cruiser to its hull speed.

However, since that effort for the short pulse is followed by a comparatively lengthy period of nil output, even the powerful radar transmitters get away with using relatively little current. The formula is:

$$\text{Mean power} = \frac{\text{Pulse duration} \times \text{Pulse power}}{\text{Pulse recurrence time}}$$

Pulse recurrence time t_i is the reciprocal of pulse repetition frequency referred to μs. For example, take the Decca 110 with 3 kHz (3000/s) pulse repetition frequency and 0.08 μs pulse duration:

$$t_i = \frac{10^6}{3000/s} 333.33\mu s$$

The operating cycle = pulse duration/t_i is then

$$z = \frac{0.08\mu s}{333.33 \ \mu s} = 2.4 \times 10^{-4}$$

But that is also the figure for the relationship between mean and peak power, and if the peak power of a set is given as 3 kW thcn the mean power of this transmitter on short range setting comes out at

$$P_m = 2.4 \times 10^{-4} \times 3000 \ W = 0.72 \ W.$$

But 1 W equals 1 volt × 1 ampere. If the set is on a 24 V supply, the average current consumption of the transmitter would thus be 0.72 VA : 24 V = 0.03 A. Actually you don't get away quite as cheaply as that, because resistances convert a portion of the current flowing into heat before it is able to produce power. The scanner motor and torque for the VDU deflection coil, the latter's cathode, and the receiver also consume current.

The Radar Lobe

The horizontal radiation from a radar scanner into free space, as far as energy distribution is concerned, is indeed club shaped. And from the edges of the parabolic-mirror scanners there are then additionally two or three pairs of side lobes, so that a largish ship close by is made to look like a small fleet of three or five vessels assembled around your own ship equidistant from it. The side lobes from a slot scanner are so insignificant that you do not get that sort of ship-multiplication from them.

Actually the boundaries of a radar beam as regards length and breadth are by no means as clear as is shown in Fig.53; the lobe outlines shade off gently. The power is bunched most strongly along the lobe axis but decreases in inverse proportion to the square of the distance from the scanner; i.e. the power around the lobe axis at a distance of 2 nm from the scanner is only one-quarter of that measured at 1 nm from it. The field strength decreases in inverse proportion to the distance from the scanner; at a distance of 2 nm it is thus only half of what it is at 1 nm. At right angles to the lobe axis the radiation power decreases very rapidly.

But of course the manufacturers like to impress their prospective clients with how well they have succeeded in focusing the radiated power, and achieve this by quoting an angular measurement. Since the outlines of the lobe are blurred, agreement has been reached to run the legs of this focusing-angle along the half-power line. Half the radiated power corresponds to a field strength reduced to 71% and an attenuation of –3 dB (decibels). A field strength down to 50% and quarter-power corresponds to –6 dB.

Beam width thus means the angle with its apex at the scanner and its legs running through the –3 dB points; it is not as large as in the lobe-caricature in Fig.53, but rather of the order of 2.2° down to 1.2°, depending on the size of the scanner. Due to this scattering angle, in fact more pulses strike a target per degree of scanner rotation than we had calculated earlier for a rotation rate of 15/min; that 8.89/deg. multiplied by a scattering angle of 1.8° comes to 16 pulses per degree.

Vertical focusing is intentionally limited to 15–30°, so that the equipment continues to function when the ship is rolling. That is why the slot scanner has upright slots—true lobe-shaped radiation requires holes in the wave guide instead of slots.

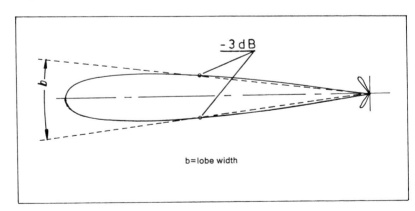

b=lobe width

Radar Horizon

The radiation from a radar is diffracted somewhat more strongly than is light in the layers of air near the ground, so that the radar horizon is somewhat beyond the visual one, namely for a scanner at height h

$d/nm = 2.21\sqrt{h/m}.$

For the acquisition of elevated targets the formula is

$d/nm = 2.21(\sqrt{h/m} + \sqrt{H/m})$ where H = altitude of the target.

If there is a layer of warm air on top of a cold ground-level layer, assuming the scanner to be in the cold layer there can be substantial overshoot, occasionally up to several hundred nautical miles — wave guide effect. A layer of cold air flowing over a warm ground-level layer produces reduced ranges.

Fig. 53   (opposite) Definition of dimensions of radar lobe. (Lobe width exaggerated here).

Passive Safety

Our problem as regards being recognised by a large vessel in the dark or in fog is always that our boats are small, of a decidedly poor reflecting material, shaped into predominantly bulbous forms, which additionally scatter the impinging radar radiation as they reflect it and so attenuate the energy returning to the transmitter. The material I am talking about is GRP, which does not reflect any better than glass fibre reinforced with carbon or aramid fibres. Wood is scarcely any better in this respect.

Even if the water is only slightly rough, with a few white horses — what the French call a 'fine sea' — and we get within a mile of a container ship or a car ferry, we have good reason to worry; because on the PPI of the freighter or the ferry, our 'own position' is surrounded by a thick cloud of so-called echoes or sea clutter, from which even good reflectors can only be picked out with a lot of luck and concentration on the part of the observer. To achieve this, he has got to turn down the gain (volume) of the receiver, but not the brilliance which could be compared with the tonal quality (flat to sharp) or, what would be even worse, the tuning. But who is going to keep on doing that?

A strong reflection can be created with the aid of a radar reflector, a sort of cat's-eye for radar 'light' comprising sheets of metal arranged at right angles to form a so-called triple mirror. Even if incoming radiation arrives at an angle, due to multiple reflection from the insides of the respectively perpendicular 'roof' surfaces of the hollow pyramid, it is echoed out through the open base of the latter in the direction of entry. Such a reflector, suitably positioned, makes our yacht look bigger than it is — and incidentally does the same for a smooth, conical buoy which theoretically is invisible to radar.

Radar Reflectors

During the quarter-century that I have been involved in the work of the German Hydrographic Institute (DHI), we have been trying to popularise amongst yachtsmen the octagon reflector of 30 cm (12 in) side-length or 22 cm (8.5 in) radius and spherical outline. This has proved optimal in practical tests provided it is mounted high up on the masthead.

A less effective alternative is the octahedral triple reflector, which in fair weather is stowed below deck and in poor visibility hoisted to the spreader. But this has to be hoisted so that one of its triple mirrors looks up to the sky — the rain-collecting position. This method is universally popular. The most frequent mounting error is to suspend the reflector from one of its points; it looks prettier but reflects substantially nothing.

In the course of time, the DHI has developed a yacht-compatible solution, involving adequately sized, 22 cm (8.5 in) radius, triple mirrors mounted just below the masthead, where the wind sensors are, facing for'd and aft respectively; i.e. in the directions in which a sailing yacht is least reflective. Athwart, the semi-oval mast and main boom reflect adequately. Wet sails are also said to reflect; that may be true in a maritime shipping lane, but in the open sea the effect would be as useless as shining a torch on your own sails.

For motor yachts, the DHI recommends the complete octahedron in rain-collector position on a raised mounting. That will produce almost the same echo in all directions. One of the larger motor yachts with a flying bridge and equipment mast, radar, TV and radio aerial, intercom loudhailer, searchlight, windtone horns and a complete fascia of instruments obviously has enough metal high-up to produce a distinct echo in fog and a calm sea. Some time ago, as we were heading east along the northern side of the Straits of Gibraltar in a real peasouper, three contacts showed up coming towards us. I had the watch below called and lifejackets donned, for our 14 m (46 ft) plastic steamer had everything named above but no radar reflector. At a range of three miles, the fast-moving trio altered course southwards and swept past a mile away to starboard — presumably naval fast craft.

An important aspect of the triple mirrors is that the surfaces are exactly perpendicular to one another. In the case of collapsible reflectors, the precision in manufacture needed to achieve this is not something that can be had for a song.

The best reflector, in my opinion, is also the heaviest and the most expensive: the 'Lensref' from Japan. It comprises a ring of inwardly facing concave mirrors around the equator of a synthetic-material sphere, which acts as focusing lens for radar radiation (Luneberg lens) and directs it onto the ring of mirrors. These reflect it and, realigned parallel by the spherical lens and, send it back. Diameter 36 cm (14 in), weight 6.64 kg (approx 14.5 lb).

Reflecting Surface of the Triple Mirror

The reflecting power of a triple mirror is substantially greater than one would guess from its dimensions. The reflecting power along the axis of symmetry of its spatial angle (corner) is compared with the visible surface of a freely suspended sphere irradiated with the same intensity (a sphere, to eliminate any directional influences).

This radar cross-section is a function of the length a of the inside edge of the corner, and of the wavelength λ which it is to reflect.

$$A_r \simeq 4{,}2\,(a^4/\lambda^2)$$

The dimensions of a and of λ must be the same.

Because a is raised to the fourth power, a small change in the size of the reflector makes a big difference. However, that is mitigated by the wavelength being squared; if it is small its effect is to enlarge A_r. The smaller the denominator of a fraction, the larger the value of the fraction. If $a = 0.3$ m, then for $\lambda = 0.03$ m (9 GHz) the radar cross-section $A_r = 37.7$ m^2,; but for $\lambda = 0.1$ m (3 GHz) it is only 3.39 m^2. (To get the fourth power on your pocket calculator, take 4 × ln a and then press the e^x button, if there is no y^x button which would do the job more quickly.)

All small-craft radars nowadays work in the 9 GHz region (X-band, 3-cm-wave). Large vessels with generous and safety-conscious owners mostly have two radars; one 3-cm wave set for its good distant resolution, and one 10-cm wave set for its deeper penetration into rain, hail and snow showers.

Transponder

Electronics D-I-Yers with the knowledge of a hacker are fully capable of constructing a transponder and fitting it in their boat where it will then operate like a Racon beacon. However, they would not get a licence for the transmitter, and if even a mere handful of pirate Racon yachts were to appear, this would create a shambles in the yacht harbours, because just ten or so would be enough to upset the whole business of taking bearings by radar.

Collision Warning Device

Many small radars — and certainly the larger ones — nowadays embody adjustable warning sectors and distances, which when switched on emit an acoustic warning signal if a vessel enters the guard-zone. You need to enquire whether only ships whose radar is switched on are reported, or all ships, which presupposes that your own radar is taking bearings and sucking operating current from the battery.

To avoid every gash-barge that passes through the guard-zone on nothing like a collision course turning the night's sleep into a sleepless night, it looks as if that alarm system will also have to have a trace discriminator. Its cost is obviously going up and up. All the same, under way with only one watchkeeper it is a useful system; at anchor perhaps just a disturbance.

In Fog: get out of the fairway
The best passive safety move in fog is to 'chicken out' from the heavy traffic and anchor outside the fairway, in the shallower water which the big boys fear, until it is all over. Particularly in the very busy regions such as the Straits of Dover, the German Bight, the Kiel Firth, at night or in poor visibility large vessels have quite enough of their own kind on the PPI to keep their eyes and ears occupied. Without radar we anyway have next to no idea of the whereabouts of that character who is hooting, or of his course — and sometimes we are not even sure of being where we think we are.

Accident Prevention

The motors of rotating scanners are powerful enough to keep them turning at the specified rate even at wind speeds of 80 kn. They are thus quite capable of sweeping overboard or knocking out someone they catch by surprise. For that reason, before anyone ever starts working on or near the scanner, put up a notice near the main switch saying 'Do Not Switch On! Danger!'.

No layman should ever be allowed to open the casing of a switched-on radar set, for inside these there are parts without any special identification at a voltage certain to kill. It is furthermore my advice to anyone who has anything to do with radio or radar, never to touch these when barefoot or stocking-footed, but rather to stick to the safety regulations drummed into every apprentice electrician: even on the most expensive carpet, electricians *never* take their shoes off. Even a poor insulator (leather soles) provides a better chance of survival than none at all. There is always a chance that an electrical defect in a set will also become a frame or casing earth fault.

Rather like a microwave oven, the radar scanner emits short-wave electromagnetic energy which starts all molecules moving so that internal and inter-molecular friction heats them up. The quickest to heat up are biological substances with poor thermal conductivity, such as butter or the vitreous body in our eyes, which as a result becomes dim and opaque. For that reason it is inadvisable to watch a rotating small-radar scanner of up to 2 m (6 ft) span from a distance of less than 1 m (3 ft). for more than 30 seconds. It will not quite make you go blind, but it will dim your sight. The vitreous body of the eye is man's most sensitive part as regards radar damage. The handful of gents who took panic flight from the flying bridge as soon as I switched on its radar need not have worried about their testicles and offspring. Unless you were to straddle a radar slot scanner for a merry-go-round joy-ride, you have nothing to worry about concerning your biological procreative potential.

When, in spite of all the croaking noises in this primer, you have acquired a radar set and gradually begun to appreciate its advantages, you may wonder what all the croaking was about. That's just the point: coupled to every technical advantage there are disadvantages which you have to get to know and learn to master. Then the advantage becomes dominant — as ever.

Which Set for What Purpose

Gert B. Büttgenbach

Types of Installation

In contrast with sets conceived for the professional navigator, there is no obligation for a yacht radar installation to undergo a type approval test on behalf of any official body before acceptance on the market and clearance for fitting on board. This means that on that part of the market where the equipment is not obligatory any set may be sold which attracts the customer, regardless of whether or not it provides in practice what the user needs. For that reason we yacht skippers must prepare ourselves particularly carefully before selecting a radar set, to avoid the disappointing discovery later that the installation does not measure up to our expectations. You have already taken the first proper step in that direction by reading this book. You know already that the performance of a radar installation depends on factors such as scanner size, transmitter pulse, peak envelope power, pulse duration, VDU picture definition, and many others. This chapter is intended to help you a little with your choice. It gives a brief picture of the various types of installation, and their suitability.

Getting Value for Money

Which one of us has not had that uncomfortable feeling you get on board, when in thick fog and under power you cross the fairway of a shipping lane or a traffic-separation zone. The hypothesis that in this situation there will be someone on board every radar-equipped ship keeping an eye on the VDU and following the echoes on its screen is no great comfort. The desire to be able to keep track of the traffic situation on your own radar screen is probably the principal reason for acquiring a radar set.

Radar sets quite good enough to allow you to avoid collisions in extensive inland waters or on the high seas are nowadays relatively inexpensive. A set with a small and compact scanner with a span of less than half a metre can be bought for no more than seven hundred to a thousand pounds. The transmitter power, low but nevertheless entirely adequate for a range of six nautical miles, is about a kilowatt. The VDU comprises a current-economising LCD.

Apelco LDR The value-for-money start. This radar installation is a good investment for safety; it is useful in an emergency, but has limited usefulness for navigation.

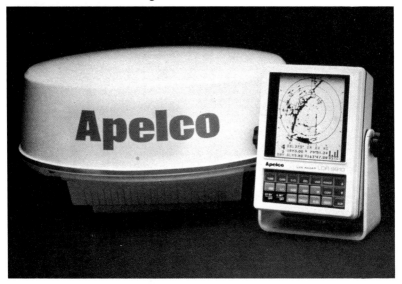

The small dimensions and affordability of this installation are what have really made radar popular on board yachts in the last few years. The power consumption of no more than 30 W makes the set practicable even for small sailing boats. In the cause of safety, this type of radar set is a good investment. No longer are skipper and crew at the mercy of the alertness of other watchkeepers in poor visibility. Should the Decca-navigator, Loran or GPS break down, with a little practice you will succeed in finding a fairway landfall-buoy. Wherever the problem is one of locating individual objects in the open sea, these sets are perfectly acceptable as a first-time radar outfit. In emergency, they will help with making landfall and avoiding collision. However, for use as navigation sets, offering independence in all kinds of waters, they are not suitable owing to the beam width of 6 degrees resulting from the short length of the scanner.

We Become More Exacting: Radar Navigation

Anyone wanting to take his motor or sailing yacht down to the Mediterranean who considers the associated problems, becomes aware of the gaps in the hyperbolic navigation system coverage of that sea area. The Decca-navigator is used only in heavily populated waters like the Straits of Gibraltar, and the Loran system does not quite cover all of the Med. For that reason the radar set as the sole autonomous navigation equipment is much more widely fitted on board yachts there than in North European waters.

However, before a radar installation can measure up to the requirements of navigation equipment, it has to meet some basic preconditions which raise its performance characteristics significantly above those of the most inexpensive class of equipment.

For a start, there is the scanner: its span should not be less than 65 cm (2 ft). That guarantees a beam width of no more than 4 degrees. Aerials of that size are encapsulated in a radome, in contrast to scanners whose span exceeds 90 cm (3 ft) which are supplied in rotating-in-the-open form. Your basic aim when buying a radar should be the largest scanner-span that your boat can accommodate. Even with beam-focusing down to 4 degrees it is not possible to identify the 100 m (328 ft) wide entrance to a harbour from as little as one mile out, whereas with a 1.20 m (4 ft) span and

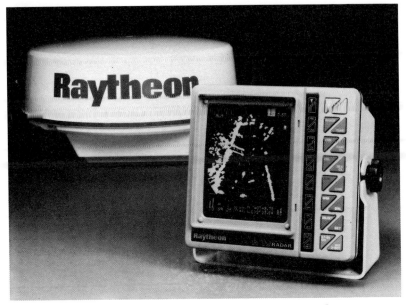

Raytheon R10 Radar as a reliable tool for the navigator. Scanners with one metre (three foot) or longer span guarantee clear radar pictures. Peak pulse powers of 4kW or more make ranges of over 20 nm possible.

focusing down to 2 degrees there should be no problem about this.

The transmitter power of this class of set, costing upwards of £2,000, will not be less than 3 kW — and for a maximum range of 20 nm you need that. The increasing importance of Racon signals lends added weight to this point. For instance, leaving the mouth of the Weser on the way to Heligoland and wanting to get fixes from Racon signals, you could not expect to get an answer from the Elbe–1 lightship Racon beacon with a mere one kilowatt of transmitter power.

Facilities that make life easier for the radar navigator in this class are already provided as standard. A variable range marker permits the precise measurement of echo ranges. The bearing graticule that can be faded-in helps to determine relative bearings. Some sets embody a warning ring, or allow this to be bought as an extra.

Koden MD3000 North-up is becoming popular: the electronic magnetic compass stabilises the radar picture; automatic plotting eases the navigator's burden and reveals collision situations.

The picture definition of the viewing screen remains a critical matter. Make a point of checking that, looking from a comfortable distance, you do not get any significant steps in the range rings. The number of picture points should not be less than 500, in both the horizontal and the vertical.

The More Elevated Class
You may already have wondered why, particularly on inland waterways, you encounter vessels with radar sets having truly monstrous scanners, whereas the dimensions of the scanner on a coastal fishing cutter are pretty modest in comparison. The reason is the improved azimuthal resolution of the radar picture as the scanner span increases — a point of particular importance in restricted waters. The trend towards longer scanners, at least 90 cm (3 ft) and up to 1.8 m (6 ft) in length, is also unmistakable in

yacht radars of the upper class costing £3,500 or more. Only these sets permit precise navigation when approaching a harbour. You can distinguish buoys clearly from larger size objects such as large vessels. Coastal outlines show up distinctly more clearly and even a narrow mole-opening presents no problem. For that reason, in this price-range you will look in vain for a so-called compact scanner with a span of less than 1 m.

Transmitter power now is raised to 4–6 kW. The longer range potential of these sets justifies the fitting of measurement arrangements out to 60 nm. The danger of multiple deflections, furthermore, means that these sets have to have finer grading of the pulse duration and pulse return, which in turn benefits the picture radial resolution, particularly at the shorter ranges of up to 2 nm.

The potential for connecting sets of this class to a gyro or electronic magnetic compass, makes it possible for the first time to orientate the radar picture not only 'head up' but also 'north up'. North stabilisation is a blessing for the radar watcher, particularly in a small craft, which because of its small mass has next to no inertia and thus is continually yawing about the course to be steered: the picture does not swing incessantly but remains still and stable. Collision threats are discovered decisive minutes sooner, since steady bearings become recognisable after only a few plottings.

In the over £5000 class there is an additional type of set on offer: analog-radar units create the picture on a CRT with long afterglow, just as they used to do forty years ago. The low luminosity of these tubes and the picture repetition frequency of about two seconds (one scanner revolution) means that viewing in daylight is only possible with a light-excluding hood. Nevertheless these sets have a significant advantage over the digital ones, which build up their picture in a video store and then display it on a monitor suitable also for daylight viewing: the definition of an analog-radar picture compares with that of a digital picture roughly as that of a photograph with that of a television screen. Faint echoes, produced by small or poorly reflecting objects, are easily distinguishable from the echoes of larger, strongly-reflecting objects.

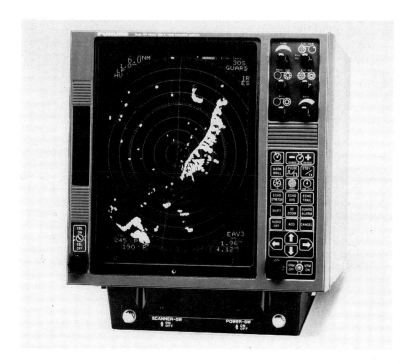

Furuno FR–8050DA This can stand up to professional scrutiny. It has stepped pulse duration, high picture definition, 10kW peak pulse power, $1\frac{1}{4}$ metre (4-foot) scanner with focusing down to 1.8 degrees.

The Outsider: Colour Radar

In the £2000 and upwards price range, colour display scopes are on offer in competition with the sets with monochrome, usually green or amber, VDUs. A distinction must be made here between two differing forms of presentation. Units that allocate a fixed colour to a given echo intensity (e.g. red for strong echoes, green for fainter ones) are scarcely to be had for less than £5000. This type of set has so far been unable to establish itself in practice, because the eye of the radar observer, tired out by hours of watchkeeping in fog, is rapidly overtaxed by the very unsettled picture.

Then there are display scopes which allocate individual colours to different information levels. For instance, the radar picture itself is green, the VRM and the bearing line white or orange. But here again, if you look carefully you will notice that the definition of colour picture tubes is greatly inferior to that of monochrome ones. Frequently, a strong flicker can be observed. And do not forget the high current consumption required for a set of this type.

The Future of Yacht Radar

With the introduction of GPS, a satellite navigation system which makes possible fixes worldwide with accuracies of the order of a metre, radar will lose its significance as an aid to coastal navigation. But there will still be nothing to replace it when it is a matter of avoiding collision in poor visibility. In the big-ship business, systems which make automatic target-following possible (ARPA — Automatic Radar Plotting Aid) have already been available for more than ten years. As semiconductor technology advances further, it is only a matter of time before the recreational skipper also needs only to mark an echo on his radar screen with a cursor, to be informed about the course and speed of the acquired ship by the radar set's computer after only a short wait.

Operation will be made even easier. Some sets no longer have keys; touching selection pads directly on the screen replaces keying. The radar picture becomes metamorphosed into the ship's data centre. Information about course, speed and machinery is displayed. Waypoints fed in by the satellite navigator appear as target markers on the display scope.

The radar of the future. Partially already realised: the radar picture
as information centre for course, speed, engine data and automatic
collision-danger recognition. A touch on the screen is enough to
mark an echo. It is economical power-wise, portable and linked to
the other navigation equipment on board.

Coastlines from the data bank of an electronic chart turn the task of comparing the radar picture with coastal formations into child's play. The radar installations become portable and grow with the requirements of their users. Fitting of an insert card suffices to turn the radar screen into an electronic chart.

All these developments will ensure that radar will have a decisive influence on the running of ships until well beyond the end of the century. Anyone still mistrusting electronics on board overlooks the fact that the dam was breached long ago. No-one in his senses would today get the idea into his head of calling a VHF/RT installation useless — in an emergency it saves lives. The Decca-navigator also has contributed considerably to safety on board. The spread of radar to yachts has created a new partnership between large craft and small craft, to the advantage of both: to see and be seen.

Index